Chimney-Pot Papers
by Charles S. Brooks.
Illustrated with wood-cuts
by Fritz Endell.

LVX ET VERITAS

1 · 9 · 2 · 0

New Haven: Yale University Press·
London: Humphrey Milford: Oxford University Press

Copyright, 1919, by
Yale University Press.

First published, 1919.
Second printing, 1920.

Publisher's Note:

The Yale University Press makes grateful acknowledgment to the Editors of the *Unpopular Review* and *The Century Magazine* for permission to include in the present volume, essays of which they were the original publishers.

To Minerva, my Wife.

Contents.

The Chimney-Pots.

M Y windows look across the roofs of the crowded city and my thoughts often take their suggestion from the life that is manifest at my neighbors' windows and on these roofs.

Across the way, one story lower than our own, there dwells "with his subsidiary parents" a little lad who has been ill for several weeks. After his household is up and dressed I regularly discover him in bed, with his books and toys piled about him. Sometimes his knees are raised to form a snowy mountain, and he leads his paper soldiers up the slope. Sometimes his kitten romps across the coverlet and pounces on his wriggling toes; and again sleeps on the sunny window-sill. His book, by his rapt attention, must deal with far-off islands and with waving cocoa-nut trees. Lately I have observed that a yellow drink is brought to him in the afternoon—a delicious blend of eggs and milk—and by the zest with which he licks the remainder from his lips, it is a prime favorite of his. In these last few days, however, I have seen the lad's nose flat and eager on the window, and I know that he is convalescent.

At another set of windows—now that the days are growing short and there is need of lights—I see in shadowgraph against the curtains an occasional domestic drama. Tonight, by the appearance of hurry and the shifting of garments, I surmise that there is preparation for a party. Presently, when the upstairs lights have disappeared, I shall see these folk below, issuing from their door in glossy raiment. My dear sir and madame, I wish you an agreeable dinner and—if your tooth resembles mine—ice-cream for dessert.

The window of a kitchen, also, is opposite, and I often look on savory messes as they ripen on the fire— a stirring with a long iron spoon. This spoon is of such unusual length that even if one supped with the devil (surely the fearful adage cannot apply to our quiet street) he might lift his food in safety from the common pot.

A good many stories lower there is a bit of roof that is set with wicker furniture and a row of gay plants along the gutter. Here every afternoon exactly at six—the roof being then in shadow—a man appears and reads his evening paper. Later his wife joins him and they eat their supper from a tray. They are sunk almost in a well of buildings which, like the hedge of a fairy garden, shuts them from all contact with the world. And here they sit when the tray has been removed. The twilight falls early at their level and, like cottagers in a valley, they watch the daylight that still gilds the peaks above them.

There is another of these out-of-door rooms above me on a higher building. From my lower level I can

see the bright canvas and the side of the trellis that
supports it.   Here, doubtless, in the cool breeze of
these summer evenings, honest folk sip their coffee
and watch the lights start across the city.

Thus, all around, I have glimpses of my neighbors—a form against the curtains—a group, in the
season, around the fire—the week's darning in a
rocker—an early nose sniffing at the open window
the morning airs.

But it is these roofs themselves that are the general
prospect.

Close at hand are graveled surfaces with spouts
and whirling vents and chimneys.   Here are posts
and lines for washing, and a scuttle from which once
a week a laundress pops her head.   Although her
coming is timed to the very hour—almost to the
minute—yet when the scuttle stirs it is with an appearance of mystery, as if one of the forty thieves
were below, boosting at the rocks that guard his cave.
But the laundress is of so unromantic and jouncing
a figure that I abandon the fancy when no more than
her shoulders are above the scuttle.   She is, however,
an amiable creature and, if the wind is right, I hear
her singing at her task.   When clothespins fill her
mouth, she experiments with popular tunes.   One
of these wooden bipeds once slipped inside and nearly
strangled her.

In the distance, on the taller buildings, water tanks
are lifted against the sky.   They are perched aloft

on three fingers, as it were, as if the buildings were just won to prohibition and held up their water cups in the first excitement of a novice to pledge the cause. Let hard liquor crouch and tremble in its rathskeller below the sidewalk! In the basement let musty kegs roll and gurgle with hopeless fear! *Der Tag!* The roof, the triumphant roof, has gone dry.

This range of buildings with water tanks and towers stops my gaze to the North. There is a crowded world beyond—rolling valleys of humanity—the heights of Harlem—but although my windows stand on tiptoe, they may not discover these distant scenes.

On summer days these roofs burn in the sun and spirals of heat arise. Tar flows from the joints in the tin. Tar and the adder—is it not a bright day that brings them forth? Now washing hangs limp upon the line. There is no frisk in undergarments. These stockings that hang shriveled and anæmic—can it be possible that they once trotted to a lively tune, or that a lifted skirt upon a crosswalk drew the eye? The very spouts and chimneys droop in the heavy sunlight. All the spinning vents are still. On these roofs, as on a steaming altar, August celebrates its hot midsummer rites.

But in winter, when the wind is up, the roofs show another aspect. The storm, in frayed and cloudy garment, now plunges across the city. It snaps its boisterous fingers. It pipes a song to summon rowdy companions off the sea. The whirling vents hum shrilly to the tune. And the tempests are roused, and the windy creatures of the hills make answer. The towers—even the nearer buildings—are obscured. The sky is gray with rain. Smoke is torn from the chimneys. Down below let a fire be snug upon the hearth and let warm folk sit and toast their feet! Let shadows romp upon the walls! Let the andirons wink at the sleepy cat! Cream or lemon, two lumps or one. Here aloft is brisker business. There is storm upon the roof. The tempest holds a carnival. And the winds pounce upon the smoke as it issues from the chimney-pots and wring it by the neck as they bear it off.

And sometimes it seems that these roofs represent youth, and its purpose, its ambition and adventure. For, from of old, have not poets lived in garrets? And are not all poets young even if their beards are white? Round and round the poet climbs, up these bare creaking flights to the very top. There is a stove to be lighted—unless the woodbox fails—a sloping ceiling and a window huddled to the floor. The poet's fingers may be numb. Although the inkpot be full, his stomach may be empty. And yet from this window, lately, a poem was cast upward to the moon. And youth and truth still rhyme in these upper rooms. Linda's voice is still the music of a sonnet. Still do

the roses fade, and love is always like the constant
stars.   And once, this!—surely from a garret:

> When I behold, upon the night's starr'd face,
> Huge cloudy symbols of a high romance,
> And think that I may never live to trace
> Their shadows, with the magic hand of chance—

Poor starved wretches are we who live softly in the
lower stories, although we are fat of body.

If a mighty pair of shears were to clip the city
somewhere below these windy gutters would there not
be a dearth of poems in the spring? Who then
would be left to note the changing colors of the twilight and the peaceful transit of the stars? Would
gray beech trees in the winter find a voice? Would
there still be a song of water and of wind? Who
would catch the rhythm of the waves and the wheat
fields in the breeze? What lilts and melodies would
vanish from the world! How stale and flat the city
without its roofs!

But it is at night that these roofs show best.   Then,
as below a philosopher in his tower, the city spreads
its web of streets, and its lights gleam in answer to
the lights above.   Galileo in his tower—Teufelsdröckh at his far-seeing attic window—saw this
glistening pageantry and had thoughts unutterable.

In this darkness these roofs are the true suburb of
the world—the outpost—the pleasant edge of our
human earth turned up toward the barren moon.

Chimneys stand as sentinels on the border of the sky. Pointed towers mark the passage of the stars. Great buildings are the cliffs on the shores of night. A skylight shows as a pleasant signal to guide the wandering skipper of the moon.

The Quest of the Lost Digamma.

MANY years ago there was a club of college undergraduates which called itself the Lost Digamma. The digamma, I am informed, is a letter that was lost in prehistoric times from the Greek alphabet. A prudent alphabet would have offered a reward at once and would have beaten up the bushes all about, but evidently these remedies were neglected. As the years went on the other letters gradually assumed its duties. The philological chores, so to speak, night and morning, that had once fallen to the digamma, they took upon themselves, until the very name of the letter was all but lost.

Those who are practiced in such matters—humped men who blink with learning—claim to discover evidence of the letter now and then in their reading. Perhaps the missing letter still gives a false quantity to a vowel or shifts an accent. It is remembered, as it were, by its vacant chair. Or rather, like a ghost it haunts a word, rattling a warning lest we disarrange a syllable. Its absence, however, in the flesh, despite the lapse of time—for it went off long ago when the mastodon still wandered on the pleasant upland—its continued absence vexes the learned. They scan ancient texts for an improper syllable and mark the time upon their brown old fingers, if possibly a jolting measure may offer them a clue. Although it must appear that the digamma—if it yet rambles alive somewhere beneath the moon—has by this time grown a beard and is lost beyond recognition, still old gentlemen meet weekly and read papers to one another on the progress of the search. Like the old woman of the story they still keep a light burning in their study windows against the wanderer's return.

Now it happened once that a group of undergraduates, stirred to sympathy beyond the common usage of the classroom, formed themselves into a club to aid in the search. It is not recorded that they were the deepest students in the class, yet mark their zeal! On a rumor arising from the chairman that the presence of the lost digamma was suspected the group rushed together of an evening, for there was an instinct that the digamma, like the raccoon, was easiest trapped at night. To stay their stomachs against a protracted search, for their colloquies sat late, they ordered a plentiful dinner to be placed before them. Also, on the happy chance that success might crown the night, a row of stout Tobies was set upon the board. If the prodigal lurked without and his vagrant nose were seen at last upon the window, then musty liquor, from a Toby's three-cornered hat, would be a fitting pledge for his return.

I do not know to a certainty the place of these meetings, but I choose to fancy that it was an upper room in a modest restaurant that went by the name of Mory's—not the modern Mory's that affects the manners of a club, but the original Temple Bar, remembered justly for its brown ale and golden bucks.

There was, of course, a choice of places where the Lost Digamma might have pushed its search. Waiving Billy's and the meaner joints conferred on freshmen, there was, to be sure, the scholastic murk of Traeger's—one room especially at the rear with steins around the walls. There was Heublein's, also. Even the Tontine might rouse a student. But I choose to consider that Mory's was the place.

Never elsewhere has cheese sputtered on toast with such hot delight. Never have such fair round eggs perched upon the top. The hen who laid the golden egg—for it could be none other than she who worked the miracle at Mory's—must have clucked like a braggart when the smoking dish came in. The dullest nose, even if it had drowsed like a Stoic through the day, perked and quivered when the breath came off the kitchen. Ears that before had never wiggled to the loudest noise came flapping forward when the door was opened. Or maybe in those days your wealth, huddled closely through the week, stretched on Saturday night to a mutton chop with bacon on the side. This chop, named of the southern downs, was so big that it curled like an anchovy to get upon the plate. The sheep that bore it across the grassy moors must have out-topped the horse. The hills

must have shaken beneath his tread.   With what
eagerness you squared your lean elbows for the feast,
with knife and fork turned upwards in your fists!

But chops in these modern days are retrograde.
Sheep have fallen to a decadent race.   Cheese has lost
its cunning.   Someone, alas, as the story says, has
killed the hen that laid the golden egg.   Mory's is
sunk and gone.   Its faded prints of the Old Brick
Row, its tables carved with students' names, its brown
Tobies in their three-cornered hats, the brasses of the
tiny bar, the rickety rooms themselves—these rise
from the past like genial ghosts and beckon us
toward pleasant memories.

Such was the zeal in those older days which the
members of the Lost Digamma spent upon their quest
that belated pedestrians—if the legend of the district
be believed—have stopped upon the curb and have
inquired the meaning of the glad shouts that issued
from the upper windows, and they have gone off
marveling at the enthusiasm attendant on this high
endeavor.   It is rumored that once when the excitement of the chase had gone to an unusual height and
the students were beating their Tobies on the table,
one of them, a fellow of uncommon ardor, lunging
forward from his chair, got salt upon the creature's
tail.   The exploit overturned the table and so rocked
the house that Louis, who was the guardian of the
place, put his nose above the stairs and cooled the
meeting.   Had it not been for his interference—he

was a good-natured fellow but unacquainted with the frenzy that marks the scholar—the lost digamma might have been trapped, to the lasting glory of the college.

As to the further progress of the club I am not informed. Doubtless it ran an honorable course and passed on from class to class the tradition of its high ambition, but never again was the lost digamma so nearly in its grasp. If it still meets upon its midnight labors, a toothless member boasts of that night of its topmost glory, and those who have gathered to his words rap their stale unprofitable mugs upon the table.

It would be unjust to assume that you are so poor a student as myself. Doubtless you are a scholar and can discourse deeply of the older centuries. You know the ancient works of Tweedledum and can distinguish to a hair's breadth 'twixt him and Tweedledee. Learning is candy on your tooth. Perhaps you stroke your sagacious beard and give a nimble reason for the lightning. To you the hills have whispered how they came, and the streams their purpose and ambition. You have studied the first shrinkage of the earth when the plains wrinkled and broke into mountain peaks. The mystery of the stars is to you as familiar as your garter. If such depth is yours, I am content to sit before you like a bucket below a tap.

At your banquet I sit as a poor relation. If the viands hold, I fork a cold morsel from your dish. . . .

But modesty must not gag me. I do myself somewhat lean towards knowledge. I run to a dictionary on a disputed word, and I point my inquiring nose upon the page like a careful schoolman. On a spurt I pry into an uncertain date, but I lack the perseverance and the wakefulness for sustained endeavor. To repair my infirmity, I frequently go among those of steadier application, if haply their devotion may prove contagious. It was but lately that I dined with a group of the Cognoscenti. There were light words at first, as when a juggler carelessly tosses up a ball or two just to try his hand before he displays his genius—a jest or two, into which I entered as an equal. In these shallow moments we waded through our soup. But we had hardly got beyond the fish when the company plunged into greater depth. I soon discovered that I was among persons skilled in those economic and social studies that now most stir us. My neighbor on the left offered to gossip with me on the latest evaluations and eventuations—for such were her pleasing words—in the department of knowledge dearest to her. While I was still fumbling for a response, my neighbor on the right, abandoning her meat, informed me of the progress of a survey of charitable organizations that was then under way. By mischance, however, while flipping up the salad on my fork, I dropped a morsel on the cloth, and I was so intent in manœuvring my plates and spoons to cover up the speck, that I lost a good part of her improving discourse.

I was still, however, making a tolerable pretense of attention, when a learned person across the table was sharp enough to see that I was a novice in the gathering. For my improvement, therefore, he fixed his great round glasses in my direction. In my confusion they seemed burning lenses hotly focused on me. Under such a glare, he thought, my tender sprouts of knowledge must spring up to full blossom.

When he had my attention, he proceeded to lay out the dinner into calories, which I now discovered to be a kind of heat or nutritive unit. He cast his appraisal on the meat and vegetables, and turned an ear toward the pantry door if by chance he might catch a hint of the dessert for his estimate, but by this time, being overwrought, I gave up all pretense, and put my coarse attention on my plate.

Sometimes I fall on better luck. It was but yesterday that I sat waiting for a book in the Public Library, when a young woman came and sat beside me on the common bench. Immediately she opened a monstrous note-book, and fell to studying it. I had myself been reading, but I had held my book at a stingy angle against the spying of my neighbors. As the young woman was of a more open nature, she laid hers out flat. It is my weakness to pry upon another's book. Especially if it is old and worn—a

musty history or an essay from the past—I squirm
and edge myself until I can follow the reader's thumb.

At the top of each page she had written the title
of a book, with a space below for comment, now well
filled. There were a hundred of these titles, and all
of them concerned John Paul Jones. She busied herself scratching and amending her notes. The whole
was thrown into such a snarl of interlineation, was so
disfigured with revision, and the writing so started
up the margins to get breath at the top, that I wondered how she could possibly bring a straight narra-
tive out of the confusion. Yet here was a book
growing up beneath my very nose. If in a year's
time—or perhaps in a six-month, if the manuscript
is not hawked too long among publishers—if when
again the nights are raw, a new biography of John
Paul Jones appears, and you cut its leaves while your
legs are stretched upon the hearth, I bid you to recog-
nize as its author my companion on the bench. Although she did not have beauty to rouse a bachelor,
yet she had an agreeable face and, if a soft white
collar of pleasing fashion be evidence, she put more
than a scholar's care upon her dress.

I am not entirely a novice in a library. Once I
gained admittance to the Reading Room of the Brit-
ish Museum—no light task even before the war.
This was the manner of it. First, I went among the
policemen who frequent the outer corridors, and inquired for a certain office which I had been told con-

trolled its affairs. The third policeman had heard of
it and sent me off with directions. Presently I went
through an obscure doorway, traversed a mean hall
with a dirty gas-jet at the turn and came before a
wicket. A dark man with the blood of a Spanish
inquisitor asked my business. I told him I was a poor
student, without taint or heresy, who sought knowledge. He stroked his chin as though it were a
monstrous improbability. He looked me up and
down, but this might have been merely a secular inquiry on the chance that I carried explosives. He
then dipped his pen in an ancient well (it was from
such a dusty fount that the warrant for Saint Barthol-
omew went forth), then bidding me be careful in my
answers, he cocked his head and shut his less suspicious eye lest it yield to mercy.

He asked my name in full, middle name and all—
as though villainy might lurk in an initial—my hotel,
my length of stay in London, my residence in
America, my occupation, the titles of the books I
sought. When he had done, I offered him my age
and my weakness for French pastry, in order that
material for a monograph might be at hand if at last
I came to fame, but he silenced me with his cold eye.
He now thrust a pamphlet in my hands, and told me
to sit alongside and read it. It contained the rules
that govern the use of the Reading Room. It was
eight pages long, and intolerably dry, and towards
the end I nodded. Awaking with a start, I was about

to hold up my hands for the adjustment of the thumb screws—for I had fallen on a nightmare—when he softened. The Imperial Government was now pleased to admit me to the Reading Room for such knowledge as might lie in my capacity.

The Reading Room is used chiefly by authors, gray fellows mostly, dried and wrinkled scholars who come here to pilfer innocently from antiquity. Among these musty memorial shelves, if anywhere, it would seem that the dusty padding feet of the lost digamma might be heard. In this room, perhaps, Christian Mentzelius was at work when he heard the book-worm flap its wings.

Here sit the scholars at great desks with ingenious shelves and racks, and they write all day and copy excerpts from the older authors. If one of them hesitates and seems to chew upon his pencil, it is but indecision whether Hume or Buckle will weigh heavier on his page. Or if one of them looks up from his desk in a blurred near-sighted manner, it is because his eyes have been so stretched upon the distant centuries, that they can hardly focus on a room. If a scholar chances to sneeze because of the infection, let it be his consolation that the dust arises from the most ancient and respected authors! Pages move silently about with tall dingy tomes in their arms. Other tomes, whose use is past, they bear off to the shades below.

I am told that once in a long time a student of

fresher complexion gets in—a novitiate with the first scholastic down upon his cheek—a tender stripling on his first high quest—a broth of a boy barely off his primer—but no sooner is he set than he feels unpleasantly conspicuous among his elders. Most of these youth bolt, offering to the doorman as a pretext some neglect—a forgotten mission at a book-stall—an errand with a tailor. Even those few who remain because of the greater passion for their studies, find it to their comfort to break their condition. Either they put on glasses or they affect a limp. I know one persistent youth who was so consumed with desire for history, yet so modest against exposure, that he bargained with a beggar for his crutch. It was, however, the rascal's only livelihood. This crutch and his piteous whimper had worked so profitably on the crowd that, in consequence, its price fell beyond the student's purse. My friend, therefore, practiced a palsy until, being perfect in the part, he could take his seat without notice or embarrassment. Alas, the need of these pretenses is short. Such is the contagion of the place—a breath from Egypt comes up from the lower stacks—that a youth's appearance, like a dyer's hand, is soon subdued to what it works in. In a month or so a general dust has settled on him. Too often learning is a Rip Van Winkle's flagon.

On a rare occasion I have myself been a student, and have plied my book with diligence. Not long ago I spent a week of agreeable days reading the many versions of Shakespeare that were played from the Restoration through the eighteenth century. They are well known to scholars, but the general reader is perhaps unfamiliar how Shakespeare was perverted. From this material I thought that I might lay out an instructive paper; how, for example, the whirling passion of Lear was once wrought to soft and pleasant uses for a holiday. Cordelia is rescued from the villains by the hero Kent, who cries out in a transport, "Come to my arms, thou loveliest, best of women!" The scene is laid in the woods, but as night comes on, Cordelia's old nurse appears. A scandal is averted. Whereupon Kent marries Cordelia, and they reign happily ever afterward. As for Lear, he advances into a gentle convalescence. Before the week is out he will be sunning himself on the bench beneath his pear tree and babbling of his early days.

There were extra witches in Macbeth. Romeo and Juliet lived and the quarreling families were united. Desdemona remained un-smothered to the end. There was one stout author—but here I trust to memory—who even attempted to rescue Hamlet and to substitute for the distant rolling of the drum of Fortinbras, the pipes and timbrels of his happy wedding. There is yet to be made a lively paper of these Shakespeare tinkers of the eighteenth century.

And then John Timbs was to have been my text, who was an antiquary of the nineteenth century. I had come frequently on his books. They are seldom found in first-hand shops. More appropriately they are offered where the older books are sold—where there are racks before the door for the rakings of the place, and inside an ancient smell of leather. If there are barrels in the basement, stocked and overflowing, it is sure that a volume of Timbs is upon the premises.

I visited the Public Library and asked a sharp-nosed person how I might best learn about John Timbs. I followed the direction of his wagging thumb. The accounts of the encyclopedias are meager, a date of birth and of death, a few facts of residence, the titles of his hundred and fifty books, and little more. Some neglect him entirely; skipping lightly from Timbrel to Timbuctoo. Indeed, Timbuctoo turned up so often that even against my intention I came to a knowledge of the place. It lies against the desert and exports ostrich feathers, gums, salts and kola-nuts. Nor are timbrels to be scorned. They were used—I quote precisely—"by David when he danced before the ark." Surely not Noah's ark! I must brush up on David.

Timbs is matter for an engaging paper. His passion was London. He had a fling at other subjects— a dozen books or so—but his graver hours were given to the study of London. There is hardly a park or square or street, palace, theatre or tavern that did not yield its secret to him. Here and there an upstart building, too new for legend, may have had no gossip

for him, but all others John Timbs knew, and the
personages who lived in them. And he knew whether
they were of sour temper, whether they were rich or
poor, and if poor, what shifts and pretenses they
practiced. He knew the windows of the town where
the beaux commonly ogled the passing beauties. He
knew the chatter of the theatres and of society. He
traced the walls of the old city, and explored the
lanes. Unless I am much mistaken, there is not a
fellow of the *Dunciad* to whom he has not assigned a
house. Nor is any man of deeper knowledge of the
clubs and coffee-houses and taverns. One would say
that he had sat at Will's with Dryden, and that he
had gone to Button's arm in arm with Addison.
Did Goldsmith journey to his tailor for a plum-
colored suit, you may be sure that Timbs tagged him
at the elbow. If Sam Johnson sat at the Mitre or
Marlowe caroused in Deptford, Timbs was of the
company. There has scarcely been a play acted in
London since the days of Burbage which Timbs did
not chronicle.

But presently I gave up the study of John Timbs.
Although I had accumulated interesting facts about
him, and had got so far as to lay out several amusing
paragraphs, still I could not fit them together to an
agreeable result. It was as though I could blow a
melodious C upon a horn, and lower down, after
preparation, a dulcet G, but failed to make a tune of
them.

But although my studies so far have been unsuccessful, doubtless I shall persist. Even now I have several topics in mind that may yet serve for pleasant papers. If I fail, it will be my comfort that others far better than myself achieve but a half success. Although the digamma escapes our salt, somewhere he lurks on the lonely mountains. And often when our lamps burn late, we fancy that we catch a waving of his tail and hear him padding across the night. But although we lash ourselves upon the chase and strain forward in the dark, the timid beast runs on swifter feet and scampers off.

On a Rainy Morning.

A NORTHEASTER blew up last night and this morning we are lashed by wind and rain. M—— foretold the change yesterday when we rode upon a 'bus top at nightfall. It was then pleasant enough and to my eye all was right aloft. I am not, however, weather-wise. I must feel the first patter of the storm before I hazard a judgment. To learn even the quarter of a breeze—unless there is a trail of smoke to guide me—I must hold up a wet finger. In my ignorance clouds sail across the heavens on a whim. Like white sheep they wander here and there for forage, and my suspicion of bad weather comes only when the tempest has whipped them to a gallop. Even a band around the moon—which I am told is primary instruction on the coming of a storm— stirs me chiefly by its deeper mystery, as if astrology, come in from the distant stars, lifts here a warning finger. But M—— was brought up beside the sea, and she has a sailor's instinct for the weather. At the first preliminary shifting of the heavens, too slight for my coarser senses, she will tilt her nose and look around, then pronounce the coming of a storm. To her, therefore, I leave all questions of umbrellas and raincoats, and on her decision we go abroad.

Last night when I awoke I knew that her prophecy

was right again, for the rain was blowing in my face and slashing on the upper window. The wind, too, was whistling along the roofs, with a try at chimney-pots and spouts. It was the wolf in the fairy story who said he'd huff and he'd puff, and he'd blow in the house where the little pig lived; yet tonight his humor was less savage. Down below I heard ash-cans toppling over all along the street and rolling to the gutters. It lacks a few nights of Hallowe'en, but doubtless the wind's calendar is awry and he is out already with his mischief. When a window rattles at this season, it is the tick-tack of his roguish finger. If a chimney is overthrown, it is his jest. Tomorrow we shall find a broken shutter as his rowdy celebration of the night.

This morning is by general agreement a nasty day. I am not sure that I assent. If I were the old woman at the corner who sells newspapers from a stand, I would not like the weather, for the pent roof drops water on her stock. Scarcely is the peppermint safe beyond the splatter. Nor is it, I fancy, a profitable day for a street-organ man, who requires a sunny morning with open windows for a rush of business. Nor is there any good reason why a house-painter should be delighted with this blustering sky, unless he is an idle fellow who seeks an excuse to lie in bed. But except in sympathy, why is our elevator boy so fiercely disposed against the weather? His cage is snug as long as the skylight holds. And why should the warm dry noses of the city, pressed against ten thousand windows up and down the streets, be flat and sour this morning with disapproval?

It may savor of bravado to find pleasure in what is so commonly condemned. Here is a smart fellow, you may say, who sets up a paradox—a conceited braggart who professes a difference to mankind. Or worse, it may appear that I try my hand at writing in a "happy vein." God forbid that I should be such a villain! For I once knew a man who, by reading these happy books, fell into pessimism and a sharp decline. He had wasted to a peevish shadow and had taken to his bed before his physician discovered the seat of his anæmia. It was only by cutting the evil dose, chapter by chapter, that he finally restored him to his friends. Yet neither supposition of my case is true. We who enjoy wet and windy days are of a considerable number, and if our voices are seldom heard in public dispute, it is because we are overcome by the growling majority. You may know us, however, by our stout boots, the kind of battered hats we wear, and our disregard of puddles. To our eyes alone, the rain swirls along the pavements like the mad rush of sixteenth notes upon a music staff. And to our ears alone, the wind sings the rattling tune recorded.

Certainly there is more comedy on the streets on a wet and windy day than there is under a fair sky. Thin folk hold on at corners. Fat folk waddle before

the wind, their racing elbows wing and wing.   Hats
are whisked off and sail down the gutters on excited
purposes of their own.   It was only this morning that
I saw an artistocratic silk hat bobbing along the pavement in familiar company with a stranger bonnet—
surely a misalliance, for the bonnet was a shabby one.
But in the wind, despite the difference of social
station, an instant affinity had been established and
an elopement was under way.

Persons with umbrellas clamp them down close
upon their heads and proceed blindly like the larger
and more reckless crabs that you see in aquariums.
Nor can we know until now what spirit for adventure
resides in an umbrella.   Hitherto it has stood in a
Chinese vase beneath the stairs and has seemed a list-
less creature.   But when a November wind is up it
is a cousin of the balloon, with an equal zest to explore
the wider precincts of the earth and to alight upon
the moon.   Only persons of heavier ballast—such as
have been fed on sweets—plump pancake persons—
can hold now an umbrella to the ground.   A long
stowage of muffins and sugar is the only anchor.

At this moment beneath my window there is a dear
little girl who brings home a package from the
grocer's.   She is tugged and blown by her umbrella,
and at every puff of wind she goes up on tiptoe.   If
I were writing a fairy tale I would make her the
Princess of my plot, and I would transport her
underneath her umbrella in this whisking wind to her

far adventures, just as Davy sailed off to the land of
Goblins inside his grandfather's clock. She would
be carried over seas, until she could sniff the spice
winds of the south. Then she would be set down in
the orchard of the Golden Prince, who presently
would spy her from his window—a mite of a pretty
girl, all mussed and blown about. And then I would
spin out the tale to its true and happy end, and they
would live together ever after. How she labors at
the turn, hugging her paper bag and holding her
flying skirts against her knees! An umbrella, however, usually turns inside out before it gets you off
the pavement, and then it looks like a wrecked Zeppe-
lin. You put it in the first ash-can, and walk off in
an attempt not to be conspicuous.

Although the man who pursues his hat is, in some
sort, conscious that he plays a comic part, and although there is a pleasing relish on the curb at his
discomfort, yet it must not be assumed that all the
humor on the street rises from misadventure. Rather,
it arises from a general acceptance of the day and a
feeling of common partnership in the storm. The
policeman in his rubber coat exchanges banter with
a cab-driver. If there is a tangle in the traffic, it
comes nearer to a jest than on a fairer day. A team-
ster sitting dry inside his hood, whistles so cheerily
that he can be heard at the farther sidewalk. Good-
naturedly he sets his tune as a rival to the wind.

It must be that only good-tempered persons are

abroad—those whose humor endures and likes the storm—and that when the swift dark clouds drove across the world, all sullen folk scurried for a roof. And is it not wise, now and then, that folk be thus parceled with their kind? Must we wait for Gabriel's Trump for our division? I have been told—but the story seems incredible—that that seemingly cursed thing, the Customs' Wharf, was established not so much for our nation's profit as in acceptance of some such general theory—in a word, that all sour persons might be housed together for their employment and society be rid of them. It is by an extension of this obscure but beneficent division that only those of better nature go abroad on these blustering November days.

There are many persons, of course, who like summer rains and boast of their liking. This is nothing. One might as well boast of his appetite for toasted cheese. Does one pin himself with badges if he plies an enthusiastic spoon in an ice-cream dish? Or was the love of sack ever a virtue, and has Falstaff become a saint? If he now sing in the Upper Choir, the bench must sag. But persons of this turn of argument make a point of their willingness to walk out in a June rain. They think it a merit to go tripping across the damp grass to inspect their gardens. Toasted cheese! Of course they like it. Who could help it? This is no proof of merit. Such folk, at best, are but sisters in the brotherhood.

And yet a November rain is but an August rain that has grown a beard and taken on the stalwart manners of the world. And the November wind, which piped madrigals in June and lazy melodies all the summer, has done no more than learn brisker braver tunes to befit the coming winter. If the wind tugs at your coat-tails, it only seeks a companion for its games. It goes forth whistling for honest celebration, and who shall begrudge it here and there a chimney if it topple it in sport?

Despite this, rainy weather has a bad name. So general is its evil reputation that from of old one of the lowest circles of Hell has been plagued with raw winds and covered thick with ooze—a testament to our northern March—and in this villains were set shivering to their chins. But the beginning of the distaste for rainy weather may be traced to Noah. Certain it is that toward the end of his cruise, when the passengers were already chafing with the animals—the kangaroos, in particular, it is said, played leap-frog in the hold and disturbed the skipper's sleep—certain it is while the heavens were still overcast that Noah each morning put his head anxiously up through the forward hatch for a change of sky. There was rejoicing from stem to stern—so runs the legend—when at last his old white beard, shifting from west to east, gave promise of a clearing wind. But from that day to this, as is natural, there has persisted a stout prejudice against wind and rain.

But this is not just. If a rainy day lacks sunshine, it has vigor for a substitute. The wind whistles briskly among the chimney tops. There is so much life on wet and windy days. Yesterday Nature yawned, but today she is wide awake. Yesterday the earth seemed lolling idly in the heavens. It was a time of celestial vacation and all the suns and moons were vacant of their usual purpose. But today the earth whirls and spins through space. Her gray cloud cap is pulled down across her nose and she leans in her hurry against the storm. The heavens have piped the planets to their work.

Yesterday the smoke of chimneys drifted up with tired content from lazy roofs, but today the smoke is stretched and torn like a triumphant banner of the storm.

"1917."

I DREAMED last night a fearful dream and this morning even the familiar contact of the subway has been unable to shake it from me.

I know of few things that are so momentarily tragical as awakening from a frightful dream. Even if you know with returning consciousness that it was a dream, it seems as if a part of it must have a basis in fact. The death that was recorded—is it true or not? And in your mind you grope among the familiar landmarks of your recollection to discover where the true and the fictitious join.

But this dream of last night was so vivid that this morning I cannot shake it from me.

I dreamed—ridiculously enough—that the whole world was at war, and that big and little nations were fighting.

In my dream the round earth hung before me

against the background of the night, and red flames shot from every part.

I heard cries of anguish—men blinded by gases and crazed by suffering. I saw women dressed in black—a long procession stretching hideously from mist to mist—walking with erect heads, dry-eyed, for grief had starved them of tears. I saw ships sinking and a thousand arms raised for a moment above the waves. I saw children lying dead among their toys.

And I saw boys throw down their books and tools and go off with glad cries, and men I saw, grown gray with despair, staggering under heavy weights.

There were millions of dead upon the earth that hung before me, and I smelled the battlefield.

And I beheld one man—one hundred men—secure in an outlawed country—who looked from far windows—men bitter with disappointment—men who blasphemed of God, while their victims rotted in Flanders.

And in my dream it seemed that I did not have a sword, but that I, too, looked upon the battle from a place where there were no flames. I ran little errands for the war.

There is the familiar window—that dull outline across the room. Here is the accustomed door. The bed is set between. It was but a dream after all. And yet how it has shaken me!

Of course the dream was absurd. No man—no

nation certainly—could be so mad. The whole whirling earth could not burn with fire. Until the final trumpet, no such calamity is possible. Thank God, it was but a dream, and I can continue today my peaceful occupation.

Calico, I'm told, is going up. I must protect our contracts.

On Going Afoot.

THERE is a tale that somewhere in the world there is a merry river that dances as often as it hears sweet music. The tale is not precise whether this river is neighbor to us or is a stream of the older world. "It dances at the noise of musick," so runs the legend, "for with musick it bubbles, dances and grows sandy." This tale may be the conceit of one of those older poets whose verses celebrate the morning and the freshness of the earth—Thomas Heywood could have written it or even the least of those poets who sat their evenings at the Mermaid— or the tale may arise more remotely from an old worship of the god Pan, who is said to have piped along the streams. I offer my credence to the earlier origin as the more pleasing. And therefore on a country walk I observe the streams if by chance any of them shall fit the tale. Not yet have I seen Pan puffing his cheeks with melody on a streamside bank—by ill luck I squint short-sightedly—but I often hear melodies of such woodsy composition that surely they must issue from his pipe. The stream leaps gaily across the shallows that glitter with sunlight, and I am tempted to the agreeable suspicion that I have hit upon the very stream of the legend and that the god Pan sits hard by in the thicket and beats his shaggy hoof in rhythm. It is his song that the wind sings in the trees. If a bird sings in the meadow its tune is pitched to Pan's reedy obligato.

Whether or not this is true, I confess to a love of a stream. This may be merely an anæmic love of beauty, such as is commonly bred in townsfolk on a holiday, or it may descend from braver ancestors who once were anglers and played truant with hook and line. You may recall that the milk-women of Kent told Piscator when he came at the end of his day's fishing to beg a cup of red cow's milk, that anglers were "honest, civil, quiet men." I have, also, a habit of contemplation, which I am told is proper to an angler. I can lean longer than most across the railing of a country bridge if the water runs noisily on the stones. If I chance to come off a dusty road—unless hunger stirs me to an inn—I can listen for an hour, for of all sounds it is the most musical. When earth and air and water play in concert, which are the master musicians this side of the moon, surely their harmony rises above the music of the stars.

In a more familiar mood I throw stepping stones in the water to hear them splash, or I cram them in a dam to thwart the purpose of the stream, laying ever a higher stone when the water laps the top. I scoop out the sand and stones as if a mighty shipping begged for passage. Or I rest from this prodigious engineering upon my back and watch the white traffic of the clouds across the summer sky. The roots of

an antique oak peep upon the flood as in the golden
days of Arden. Apple blossoms fall upon the water
like the snow of a more kindly winter. A gay leaf
puts out upon the channel like a painted galleon for
far adventure. A twig sails off freighted with my
drowsy thoughts. A branch of a willow dips in the
stream and writes an endless trail of words in the
running water. In these evil days when the whole
fair world is trenched and bruised with war, what
wisdom does it send to the valleys where men reside—
what love and peace and gentleness—what promise
of better days to come—that it makes this eternal
stream its messenger!

And yet a stream is best if it is but an incident in
travel—if it break the dusty afternoon and send one
off refreshed. Rather than a place for fishing it
invites one to bathe his feet. There are, indeed,
persons so careful of their health as to assert that cold
water endangers blisters. Theirs is a prudence to be
neglected. Such persons had better leave their feet
at home safely slippered on the fender. If one's feet
go upon a holiday, is it fair that for fear of consequence they be kept housed in their shoes? Shall the
toes sit inside their battered caravans while the legs
and arms frisk outside? Is there such torture in a
blister—even if the prevention be sure—to outweigh
the pleasure of cold water running across the ankles?

It was but lately that I followed a road that lay off
the general travel through a pleasant country of hills

and streams.   As the road was not a thoroughfare
and journeyed no farther than the near-by town
where I was to get my supper, it went at a lazy winding pace.   If a dog barked it was in sleepy fashion.
He yelped merely to check his loneliness.   There
could be no venom on his drowsy tooth.   The very
cows that fed along its fences were of a slower breed
and more contemplative whisk of tail than are found
upon the thoroughfares.   Sheep patched the fields
with gray and followed their sleepy banquet across
the hills.

The country was laid out with farms—orchards
and soft fields of grain that waved like a golden
lake—but there were few farmhouses.   In all the
afternoon I passed but one person, a deaf man who
asked for direction.   When I cried out that I was a
stranger, he held his hand to his ear, but his mouth
fell open as if my words, denied by deafness from a
proper portal, were offered here a service entrance.
I spread my map before him and he put an ample
thumb upon it.   Then inquiring whether I had
crossed a road with a red house upon it where his
friend resided, he thanked me and walked off with
such speed as his years had left him.   Birds sang
delightfully on the fences and in the field, yet I knew
not their names.   Shall one not enjoy a symphony
without precise knowledge of the instrument that
gives the tune?   If an oboe sound a melody, must one
bestow a special praise, with a knowledge of its func-

tion in the concert? Or if a trombone please, must
one know the brassy creature by its name? Rather,
whether I listen to horns or birds, in my ignorance I
bestow loosely a general approbation; yet is the song
sweet.

All afternoon I walked with the sound of wind and
water in my ears, and at night, when I had gained my
journey's end and lay in bed, I heard beneath my
window in the garden the music of a little runnel that
was like a faint and pleasant echo of my hillside walk.
I fell asleep to its soothing sound and its trickle made
a pattern across my dreams.

But perhaps you yourself, my dear sir, are addicted
to these country walks, either for an afternoon or for
a week's duration with a rucksack strapped across
your back. If denied the longer outing, I hope that
at least it is your custom to go forth upon a holiday
to look upon the larger earth. Where the road most
winds and dips and the distance is of the finer purple,
let that direction be your choice! Seek out the region
of the hills! Outposts and valleys here, with smoke
of suppers rising. Trains are so small that a child
might draw them with a string. Far-off hills are
tumbled and in confusion, as if a giant were roused
and had flung his rumpled cloak upon the plain.

Or if a road and a stream seem close companions,
tag along with them! Like three cronies you may
work the countryside together! There are old mills

with dams and mossy water wheels, and rumbling
covered bridges.

But chiefly I beg that you wander out at random
without too precise knowledge of where you go or
where you shall get your supper. If you are of a
cautious nature, as springs from a delicate stomach
or too sheltered life, you may stuff a bar of chocolate
in your pocket. Or an apple—if you shift your other
ballast—will not sag you beyond locomotion. I have
known persons who prize a tomato as offering both
food and drink, yet it is too likely to be damaged and
squirt inside the pocket if you rub against a tree.
Instead, the cucumber is to be commended for its
coolness, and a pickle is a sour refreshment that
should be nibbled in turn against the chocolate.

Food oftentimes is to be got upon the way. There
is a kind of cocoanut bar, flat and corrugated, that
may be had at most crossroads. I no longer consider
these a delicacy, but in my memory I see a boy bargaining for them at the counter. They are counted
into his dirty palm. He stuffs a whole one in his
mouth, from ear to ear. His bicycle leans against the
trough outside. He mounts, wabbling from side to
side to reach the pedals. Before him lie the mountains of the world.

Nor shall I complain if you hold roughly in your
mind, subject to a whim's reversal, an evening destination to check your hunger. But do not bend your
circuit back to the noisy city! Let your march end

at the inn of a country town! If it is but a station on
your journey and you continue on the morrow, let
there be an ample porch and a rail to rest your feet!
Here you may sit in the comfortable twilight when
crammed with food and observe the town's small
traffic. Country folk come about, if you are of easy
address, and engage you on their crops. The village
prophet strokes his wise beard at your request and,
squinting at the sky, foretells a storm. Or if the
night is cold, a fire is laid inside and a wrinkled board
for the conduct of the war debates upon the hearth.
But so far as your infirmity permits, go forth at
random with a spirit for adventure! If the prospect
pleases you as the train slows down for the platform,
cast a penny on your knee and abide its fall!

Or if on principle you abhor a choice that is made
wickedly on the falling of a coin, let an irrelevant
circumstance direct your destination! I once walked
outside of London, making my start at Dorking for
no other reason except that Sam Weller's mother-in-
law had once lived there. You will recall how the
elder Mr. Weller in the hour of his affliction dis-
coursed on widows in the taproom of the Marquis
of Granby when the funeral was done, and how later,
being pestered with the Reverend Mr. Stiggins, he
immersed him in the horse-trough to ease his grief.
All through the town I looked for red-nosed men who
might be descended from the reverend shepherd,
and once when I passed a horse-trough of uncommon

size I asked the merchant at the corner if it might
not be the very place. I was met, however, by such
a vacant stare—for the fellow was unlettered—that
to rouse him I bought a cucumber from an open crate
against the time of lunch, and I followed my pursuit
further in the town. The cucumber was of monstrous
length and thin. All about the town its end stuck out
of my pocket inquisitively, as though it were a fellow
traveler down from London to see the sights. But
although I inquired for the Weller family, it seems
that they were dead and gone. Even the Marquis of
Granby had disappeared, with its room behind the
bar where Mr. Stiggins drank pineapple rum with
water, *luke,* from the kettle on the hob.

We left Dorking and walked all afternoon through
a pleasant sunny country, up hill and down, to the
town of Guildford. At four o'clock, to break the
journey, we laid out our lunch of bread and cheese
and cucumber, and rested for an hour. The place
was a grassy bank along a road above a fertile valley
where men were pitching hay. Their shouts were
carried across the fields with an agreeable softness.
Today, doubtless, women work in those fields.

On another occasion we walked from Maidstone to
Rochester on pilgrimage to the inn where Alfred
Jingle borrowed Mr. Winkle's coat to attend the
Assembly, when he made love to the buxom widow.
War had just been declared between Britain and
Germany, and soldiers guarded the roads above the

town. At a tea-room in the outskirts army officers
ate at a neighboring table. Later, it is likely, they
were in the retreat from Mons: for the expeditionary
force crossed the channel within a week. Yet so does
farce march along with tragedy that our chief concern in Rochester was the old inn where the ball was
held.

A surly woman who sat behind the cashier's wicket
fixed me with her eye. "Might we visit the ballroom?" I inquired. Evidently not, unless we were
stopping at the house. "Madame," I said, "perhaps
you are unaware that the immortal Mr. Pickwick
once sojourned beneath your roof." There was no
response. "The celebrated Mr. Pickwick, G. C. M.
P. C.," I continued, "who was the discoverer of the
sources of the Hampstead Ponds." At this—for my
manner was impressive—she fumbled through the last
few pages of her register and admitted that he might
have been once a patron of the house, but that he had
now paid his bill and gone.

I was about to question her about the poet Augus-
tus Snodgrass, who had been with Mr. Pickwick on
his travels, when a waiter, a humorous fellow with a
vision of a sixpence, offered to be our guide. We
climbed the stairs and came upon the ballroom. It
was a small room. Three quadrilles must have
stuffed it to the edge—a dingy place with bare windows on a deserted innyard. At one end was a
balcony that would hold not more than three musi-

cians. The candles of its former brightness have
long since burned to socket. Vanished are "Sir
Thomas Clubber, Lady Clubber and the Miss
Clubbers!" Gone is the Honorable Wilmot Snipe
and all the notables that once crowded it! Vanished
is the punchbowl where the amorous Tracy Tupman
drank too many cups of negus on that memorable
night. I gave the dirty waiter a sixpence and came
away.

I discourage the usual literary pilgrimage. Indeed, if there is a rumor that Milton died in a neighboring town, or a treaty of consequence was signed
close by, choose another path! Let neither Oliver
Cromwell nor the Magna Carta deflect your course!
One of my finest walks was on no better advice than
the avoidance of a celebrated shrine. I was led along
the swift waters of a river, through several pretty
towns, and witnessed the building of a lofty bridge.
For lunch I had some memorable griddlecakes.
Finally I rode on top of a rattling stage with a gossip
for a driver, whose long finger pointed out the sights
upon the road.

But for the liveliest truancy, keep an eye out for
red-haired and freckled lads, and make them your
counselors! Lads so spotted and colored, I have
found, are of unusual enterprise in knowing the best
woodland paths and the loftiest views. A yellow-
haired boy, being of paler wit, will suck his thumb
upon a question. A touzled black exhibits a sulky

absorption in his work. An indifferent brown, at best, runs for an answer to the kitchen. But red-haired and freckled lads are alive at once. Whether or not their roving spirit, which is the basis of their deeper and quicker knowledge, proceeds from the magic of the pigment, the fact yet remains that such boys are surer than a signpost to direct one to adventure. This truth is so general that I have read the lives of the voyagers—Robinson Crusoe, Captain Kidd and the worthies out of Hakluyt—if perhaps a hint might drop that they too in their younger days were freckled and red-haired. Sir Walter Raleigh—I choose at random—was doubtless called "Carrots" by his playmates. But on making inquiry of a red-haired lad, one must have a clear head in the tumult of his direction. I was once lost for several hours on the side of Anthony's Nose above the Hudson because I jumbled such advice. And although I made the acquaintance of a hermit who dwelt on the mountain with a dog and a scarecrow for his garden—a fellow so like him in garment and in feature that he seemed his younger and cleaner brother—still I did not find the top or see the clear sweep of the Hudson as was promised.

If it is your habit to inquire of distance upon the road, do not quarrel with conflicting opinion! Judge the answer by the source! Persons of stalwart limb commonly underestimate a distance, whereas those of broken wind and stride stretch it greater than it

is. But it is best to take all answers lightly. I have
heard of a man who spent his rainy evenings on a
walking trip in going among the soda clerks and
small merchants of the village, not for information,
but to contrast their ignorance. Aladdin's wicked
uncle, when he inquired direction to the mountain of
the genii's cave, could not have been so misdirected.
Shoemakers, candy-men and peddlers of tinware—if
such modest merchants existed also on the curb in
those magic days—must have been of nicer knowledge or old Kazrac would never have found the lamp.
In my friend's case, on inquiry, a certain hotel at
which we aimed was both good and bad, open and
shut, burned and unburned.

There is a legend of the Catholic Church about a
certain holy chapel that once leaped across the Alps.
It seems gross superstition, yet although I belong
to a protesting church, I assert its likelihood. For
I solemnly affirm that on a hot afternoon I chased
a whole village that skipped quite as miraculously
before me across the country. It was a village of
stout leg and wind and, as often as I inquired, it still
kept seven miles ahead. Once only I gained, by
trotting on a descent. Not until night when the village lay down to rest beside a quiet river did I finally
overtake it. And the next morning I arose early in
order to be off first upon my travels, and so keep the
lively rascal in the rear.

In my country walks I usually carry a book in the

pocket opposite to my lunch. I seldom read it, but it is a comfort to have it handy. I am told that at one of the colleges, students of smaller application, in order that they may truthfully answer as to the length of time they have spent upon their books, do therefore literally sit upon a pile of them, as on a stool, while they engage in pleasanter and more secular reading. I do not examine this story closely, which rises, doubtless, from the jealousy of a rival college. Rather, I think that these students perch upon the books which presently they must read, on a wise instinct that this preliminary contact starts their knowledge. And therefore a favorite volume, even if unopened in the pocket, does nevertheless by its proximity color and enhance the enjoyment of the day. I have carried Howell, who wrote the "Familiar Letters," unread along the countryside. A small volume of Boswell has grown dingy in my pocket. I have gone about with a copy of Addison with long S's, but I read it chiefly at home when my feet are on the fender.

I had by me once as I crossed the Devon moors a volume of "Richard Feverel." For fifteen miles I had struck across the upland where there is scarcely a house in sight—nothing but grazing sheep and wild ponies that ran at my approach. Sometimes a marshy stream flowed down a shallow valley, with a curl of smoke from a house that stood in the hollow. At the edge of this moorland, I came into a shady valley

that proceeded to the ocean. My feet were pinched
and tired when I heard the sound of water below the
road. I pushed aside the bushes and saw a stream
trickling on the rocks. I thrust my head into a pool
until the water ran into my ears, and then sat with
my bare feet upon the cool stones where the runnel
lapped them, and read "Richard Feverel." To this
day, at the mention of the title, I can hear the pleasant brawl of water and the stirring of the branches
in the wind that wandered down the valley.

Hazlitt tells us in a famous passage with what
relish he once read "The New Eloise" on a walking
trip. "It was on the 10th of April, 1798," he writes,
"that I sat down to a volume of the New Eloise, at
the inn at Llangollen, over a bottle of sherry and a
cold chicken." I am quite unfamiliar with the book,
yet as often as I read the essay—which is the best
of Hazlitt—I have been teased to buy it. Perhaps
this springs in part from my own recollection of
Llangollen, where I once stopped on a walking trip
through Wales. The town lies on the river Dee at
the foot of fertile hills patched with fences, on whose
top there stand the ruins of Dinas Bran, a fortress
of forgotten history, although it looks grimly towards
the English marches as if its enemies came thence.
Thrown across the river there is a peaked bridge of
gray stone, many centuries old, on which the village
folk gather at the end of day. I dined on ale and
mutton of such excellence that, for myself, a cold

volume of the census—if I had fallen so low—must
have remained agreeably in memory. I recall that
a street-organ stopped beneath the window and
played a merry tune—or perhaps the wicked ale was
mounting—and I paused in my onslaught against
the mutton to toss the musician a coin.

I applaud those who, on a walking trip, arise and
begin their journey in the dawn, but although I am
eager at night to make an early start, yet I blink and
growl when the morning comes. I marvel at the poet
who was abroad so early that he was able to write of
the fresh twilight on the world—"Where the san-
dalled Dawn like a Greek god takes the hurdles of
the hills"—but for my own part I would have slept
and missed the sight. But an early hour is best, despite us lazybones, and to be on the road before the
dew is gone and while yet a mist arises from the
hollows is to know the journey's finest pleasure.

Persons of early hours assert that they feel a fine
exaltation. I am myself inclined to think, however,
that this is not so much an exaltation that arises from
the beauty of the hour, as from a feeling of superior-
ity over their sleeping and inferior comrades. It is
akin to the displeasing vanity of those persons who
walk upon a boat with easy stomach while their companions lie below. I would discourage, therefore,
persons that lean toward conceit from putting a foot
out of bed until the second call. On the other hand,
those who are of a self-depreciative nature should get

up with the worm and bird. A man of my own acquaintance who was sunk in self-abasement for many years, was roused to a salutary conceit by no other tonic.

And it is certain that to be off upon a journey with a rucksack strapped upon you at an hour when the butcher boy takes down his shutters is a high pleasure. Off you go through the village with swinging arms. Off you go across the country. A farmer is up before you and you hear his reaper across the field, and the neighing of his horses at the turn. Where the hill falls sharp against the sky, there he stands outlined, to wipe the sweat. And as your nature is, swift or sluggish thoughts go through your brain—plots and vagrant fancies, which later your pencil will not catch. It is in these earliest hours while the dew still glistens that little lyric sentences leap into your mind. Then, if at all, are windmills giants.

There are cool retreats where you may rest at noon, but Stevenson has written of these. "You come," he writes, "to a milestone on a hill, or some place where deep ways meet under trees; and off goes the knapsack, and down you sit to smoke a pipe in the shade. You sink into yourself, and the birds come round and look at you; and your smoke dissipates upon the afternoon under the blue dome of heaven; and the sun lies warm upon your feet, and the cool air visits your neck and turns aside your open shirt. If you are not happy, you must have an evil conscience."

And yet a good inn at night holds even a more tranquil joy. M—— and I, who frequently walk upon a holiday, traversed recently a mountain road to the north of West Point. During the afternoon we had scrambled up Storm King to a bare rock above the Hudson. It was just such an outlook as Rip found before he met the outlandish Dutchmen with their ninepins and flagon. We lay here above a green world that was rimmed with mountains, and watched the lagging sails and puffs of smoke upon the river. It was late afternoon when we descended to the mountain road that runs to West Point. During all the day there had been distant rumbling of thunder, as though a storm mustered in a far-off valley,—or perhaps the Dutchmen of the legend still lingered at their game,—but now as the twilight fell the storm came near. It was six o'clock when a signboard informed us that we had seven miles to go, and already the thunder sounded with earnest purpose. Far below in the dusk we saw the lights of West Point. On a sudden, while I was still fumbling for my poncho which was rolled inside my rucksack, the storm burst upon us. We put up the umbrella and held the poncho against the wind and driving rain. But the wind so whisked it about and the rain was so eager to find the openings that presently we were drenched. In an hour we came to West Point.

Luckily the cook was up, and she served us a hot dinner in our rooms with the washstand for a table. When we started there was a piece of soap in the dish, but I think we ate it in our hunger. I recall that there was one course that foamed up like custard and was not upon the bill. It was a plain room with meager furniture, yet we fell asleep with a satisfaction beyond the Cecils in their lordly beds. I stirred once when there was a clamor in the hall of guests returning from a hop at the Academy—a prattle of girls' voices—then slept until the sun was up.

But my preference in lodgings is the low sagging half-timbered building that one finds in the country towns of England. It has leaned against the street and dispensed hospitality for three hundred years. It is as old a citizen as the castle on the hill. It is an inn where Tom Jones might have spent the night, or any of the rascals out of Smollett. Behind the wicket there sits a shrewish female with a cold eye towards your defects, and behind her there is a row of bells which jangle when water is wanted in the rooms. Having been assigned a room and asked the hour of dinner, you mount a staircase that rises with a squeak. There is a mustiness about the place, which although it is unpleasant in itself, is yet agreeable in its circumstance. A long hall runs off to the back of the house, with odd steps here and there to throw you. Your room looks out upon a coach-yard, and as you wash you overhear a love-passage down below.

In the evening you go forth to see the town. If it lies on the ocean, you walk upon the mole and watch the fisher folk winding up their nets, or sitting with tranquil pipes before their doors. Maybe a booth has been set up on the parade that runs along the ocean, and a husky fellow bids you lay out a sixpence for the show, which is the very same, he bawls, as was played before the King and the Royal Family. This speech is followed by a fellow with a trombone, who blows himself very red in the face.

But rather I choose to fancy that it is an inland town, and that there is a quieter traffic on the streets. Here for an hour after dinner, while darkness settles, you wander from shop to shop and put your nose upon the glass, or you engage the lamplighter as he goes his rounds, for any bit of news.

Once in such a town when the night brought rain, for want of other employment, I debated divinity with a rigid parson, and until a late hour sat in the thick curtain of his attack. It was at an inn of one of the midland counties of England, a fine old weathered building, called "The King's Arms." In the tap—for I thrust my thirsty head inside—was an array of old pewter upon the walls, and two or three prints of prize fighters of former days. But it was in the parlor the parson engaged me. In the corner of the room there was a timid fire—of the kind usually met in English inns—imprisoned behind a grill that had been set up stoutly to confine a larger and rowdier fire. My antagonist was a tall lank man of pinched ascetic face and dark complexion, with clothes brushed to shininess, and he belonged to a brotherhood that lived in one of the poorer parts of London along the wharves. His sojourn at the inn was forced. For two weeks in the year, he explained, each member was cast out of the conventual buildings upon the world. This was done in penance, as the members of more rigid orders in the past were flagellants for a season. So here for a whole week had he been sitting, for the most part in rainy weather, busied with the books that the inn afforded— advertising booklets of the beauties of the Alps— diagrams of steamships—and peeking out of doors for a change of sky.

It was a matter of course that he should engage me in conversation. He was as lonesome for a chance to bark as a country dog. Presently when I dissented from some point in his creed, he called me a heretic, and I with gentlest satire asked him if the word yet lived. But he was not angry, and he told me of his brotherhood. It had a branch in America, and he bade me, if ever I met any of its priests, to convey to them his warm regards. As for America, it was, he said, too coldly ethical, and needed most a spiritual understanding; to which judgment I assented. I wonder now whether the war will bring that understanding. Maybe, unless blind hatred smothers it.

This priest was a mixture of stern and gentle qualities, and seemed to be descended from those earlier friars that came to England in cord and gown, and went barefoot through the cities to minister comfort and salvation to the poor and wretched. When the evening was at last spent, by common consent we took our candles on the landing, where, after he inculcated a final doctrine of his church with waving finger, he bade me good night, with a wish of luck for my journey on the morrow, and sought his room.

My own room lay down a creaking hallway. When undressed, I opened my window and looked upon the street. All lights were out. At last the rain had ceased, and now above the housetops across the way, through a broken patch of cloud, a star appeared with a promise of a fair tomorrow.

On Livelihoods.

SOMEWHERE in his letters, I think, Stevenson pronounces street paving to be his favorite occupation. I fancy, indeed,—and I have ransacked his life,—that he never applied himself to its practice for an actual livelihood. That was not necessary. Rather, he looked on at the curb in a careless whistling mood, hands deep in the pockets of his breeks, in a lazy interval between plot and essay. The sunny morning had dropped its golden invitation through his study windows, and he has wandered forth to see the world. Let my heroes—for thus I interpret him at his desk as the sunlight beckoned—let my heroes kick their heels in patience! Let villains fret inside the inkpot! Down, sirs, down, into the glossy magic pool, until I dip you up! Pirates—for surely such miscreants lurked among his papers—let pirates, he cries, save their red oaths until tomorrow! My hat! My stick!

It was thus, then, as an amateur that Stevenson looked on street paving—the even rows of cobbles, the nice tapping to fit the stones against the curb, the neat joint around the drain. And yet, unpardonably, he neglects the tarpot; and this seems the very soul of the business, the finishing touch—almost culinary, as when a cook pours on a chocolate sauce.

I remember pleasantly when our own street was paved. There had been laid a waterpipe, deep down where the earth was yellow—surely gold was near— and several of us young rascals climbed in and out in the twilight when work was stopped. By fits we were both mountaineers and miners. There was an agreeable gassy smell as if we neared the lower regions. Here was a playground better than the building of a barn, even with its dizzy ladders and the scaffolding around the chimney. Or we hid in the great iron pipes that lay along the gutters, and followed our leader through them home from school. But when the pipes were lowered into place and the surface was cobbled but not yet sanded, then the tarpot yielded gum for chewing. At any time after supper a half dozen of us—blacker daubs against the darkness—might have been seen squatting on the stones, scratching at the tar. Blackjack, bought at the corner, had not so full a flavor. But one had to chew forward in the mouth—lightly, lest the tar adhere forever to the teeth.

And yet I am not entirely in accord with Stevenson in his preference.

And how is it, really, that people fall into their livelihoods? What circumstance or necessity drives them? Does choice, after all, always yield to a contrary wind and run for any port? Is hunger always the helmsman? How many of us, after due appraisal of ourselves, really choose our own parts in the mighty drama?—first citizen or second, with our shrill voices for a moment above the crowd—first citizen or second—brief choristers, except for vanity, against a painted scene. How runs the rhyme?— rich man, poor man, beggar man, thief; doctor, lawyer, merchant, chief! And a robustious fellow with great voice, and lace and sword, strutting forward near the lights.

Meditating thus, I frequently poke about the city in the end of afternoon "when the mind of your man of letters requires some relaxation." I peer into shop windows, not so much for the wares displayed as for glimpses of the men and women engaged in their disposal. I watch laborers trudging home with the tired clink of their implements and pails. I gaze into cellarways where tailor and cobbler sit bent upon their work—needle and peg, their world—and through fouled windows into workrooms, to learn which livelihoods yield the truest happiness. For it is, on the whole, a whistling rather than a grieving world, and like little shouts among the hills is laughter echoed in the heart.

I can well understand how one can become a baker or even a small grocer with a pencil behind his ear. I could myself honestly recommend an apple—an astrachan for sauces—or, in the season, offer asparagus with something akin to enthusiasm. Cranberries, too, must be an agreeable consort of the autumn months when the air turns frosty. I would

own a cat with a dusty nose to rub along the barrels
and sleep beneath the stove. I would carry dried
meats in stock were it only for the electric slicing
machine. And whole cheeses! Or to a man of
romantic mind an old brass shop may have its lure.
To one of musty turn, who would sit apart, there is
something to be said for the repair of violins and
'cellos. At the least he sweetens discord into melody.

But I would not willingly keep a second-hand
bookshop. It is too cluttered a business. There is
too free a democracy between good and bad. It was
Dean Swift who declared that collections of books
made him melancholy, "where the best author is as
much squeezed and as obscure as a porter at a coro-
nation." Nor is it altogether reassuring for one who
is himself by way of being an author to view the
certain neglect that awaits him when attics are
cleared at last. There is too leathery a smell upon
the premises, a thick deposit of mortality. I draw
a deep breath when I issue on the street, grateful for
the sunlight and the wind. However, I frequently
put my head in at Pratt's around the corner, sometimes by chance when the family are assembled for
their supper in one of the book alcoves. They have
swept back a litter of historians to make room for
the tray of dishes. To cut them from the shop they
have drawn a curtain in front of their nook, but I can
hear the teapot bubbling on the counter. There is,
also, a not unsavory smell which, if my old nose

retains its cunning, is potato stew, fetched up from the kitchen. If you seek Gibbon now, Pratt's face will show like a withered moon between the curtains and will request you to call later when the dishes have been cleared.

No one works in cleaner produce than carpenters. They are for the most part a fatherly whiskered tribe and they eat their lunches neatly from a pail, their backs against the wall, their broad toes upturned. I look suspiciously on painters, however, who present themselves for work like slopped and shoddy harlequins, and although I have myself passed a delightful afternoon painting a wooden fence at the foot of the garden—and been scraped afterwards—I would not wish to be of their craft.

But perhaps one is of restless habit and a peripatetic occupation may be recommended. For a bachelor of small expense, at a hazard, a wandering fruit and candy cart offers the venture and chance of unfamiliar journeys. There is a breed of lollypop on a stick that shows a handsome profit when the children come from school. Also, at this minute, I hear below me on the street the flat bell of the scissors-grinder. I know not what skill is required, yet it needs a pretty eye and even foot. The ragman takes to an ancestral business and chants the ancient song of his fathers. When distance has somewhat muffled its nearer sharpness, the song bears a melody unparalleled among tradesmen's cries. Window glass, too, is hawked pleasantly from house to house and requires but a knife and putty. In the spring the vegetable vender, standing in his wagon, utters melodious sounds that bring the housewives to their windows. Once, also, by good luck, I fell into acquaintance with a fellow who peddled brooms and dustpans along the countryside. He was hung both front and back with cheap commodities—a necklace of scrubbing brushes—tins jangling against his knees. A very kitchen had become biped. A pantry had gone on pilgrimage. Except for dogs, which seemed maddened by his strange appearance, it was, he informed me, an engaging livelihood for a man who chafed indoors. Or for one of dreamy disposition the employment of a sandwich man, with billboards fore and aft, offers a profitable repose. Sometimes several of these philosophers journey together up the street in a crowded hour, one behind another with slow introspective step, as befits their high preoccupation.

Or one has an ear, and the street-organ commends itself. Observe the musician at the corner, hat in hand and smiling! Let but a curtain stir and his eye will catch it. He hears a falling penny as 'twere any nightingale. His tunes are the herald of the gaudy spring. His are the dancing measures of the sunlight. And is anyone a surer judge of human nature? He allows dyspeptics to slink along the fence. Those of bilious aspect may go their ways unchallenged.

Spare me those, he says, who have not music in their
souls: they are fit for treasons, stratagems, and spoils.
It was with a flute that the poet Goldsmith starved
his way through France. Yet the flute is a cold un-
stirring instrument. He would have dined the oftener
had he pitched upon a street-organ.

But in this Christmas season there is a man goes
up and down among the shoppers blowing shrill
tunes upon a pipe. A card upon his hat announces
that it is music makes the home and that one of his
marvelous implements may be bought for the trifling
and altogether insignificant sum of ten cents. A
reticule across his stomach bulges with his pipes. He
seems to manipulate the stops with his fingers, but
I fancy that he does no more than sing into the larger
opening. Yet his gay tune sounds above the traffic.

I have wondered where such seasonal professions
recruit themselves. The eyeglass man still stands at
his corner with his tray. He is, moreover, too sodden
a creature to play upon a pipe. Nor is there any
dwindling of shoe-lace peddlers. The merchants of
popcorn have not fallen off in number, and peanuts
hold up strong. Rather, these Christmas musicians
are of the tribe which at other festivals sell us little
flags and bid us show our colors. They come from
country fairs and circuses. All summer long they
bid us gather for the fat man, or they cry up the
beauties of a Turkish harem. If some valiant fellow
in a painted tent is about to swallow glass, they are

his horn and drum to draw the crowd. I once knew a side-show man who bent iron bars between his teeth and who summoned stout men from his audience to swing upon the bar, but I cannot believe that he has discharged the bawling rascal at his door. I rather choose to think that the piper was one of those self-same artists who, on lesser days, squeeze comic rubber faces in their fingers, or make the monkey climb its predestined stick.

Be this as it may, presently the piper hit on a persuasive tune and I abandoned all thought of the Noah's ark—my errand of the morning for my nephew—and joined the crowd that followed him. Hamelin Town was come again. But street violins I avoid. They suggest mortgages and unpaid rent.

But with the world before him why should a man turn dentist? He must have been a cruel fellow from his rattle. When did his malicious ambition first sprout up towards molars and bicuspids? Or who would scheme to be a plumber? He is a cellarer— alas, how shrunk from former days! Or consider the tailor! Perhaps you recall Elia's estimate. "Do you ever see him," he asks, "go whistling along the footpath like a carman, or brush through a crowd like a baker, or go smiling to himself like a lover?"

Certainly I would not wish to be a bookkeeper and sit bent all day over another's wealth. I would not want to bring in on lifted fingers the meats which another eats. Nor would I choose to be a locksmith,

which is a kind of squint-eyed business, up two dismal
stairs and at the rear. A gas lamp flares at the turn.
A dingy staircase mounts into a thicker gloom. The
locksmith consorts with pawnbrokers, with cheap
sign-makers and with disreputable doctors; yet he is
not of them. For there adheres to him a sort of
romance. He is a creature of another time, set in
our midst by the merest chance. The domestic cat,
descended from the jungle, is not more shrunk. Keys
have fallen on evil days. Observe the mighty row of
them hung discarded along his boxes! Each one is fit
to unlock a castle. Warwick itself might yield to
such a weight of metal—rusty now, disused, quite out
of fashion, displaced by a race of dwarfs. In the old
prints, see how the London 'prentice runs with his
great key in the dawn to take down his master's shutter! In a musty play, observe the jailor at the dun-
geon door! Without massive keys jingling at the
belt the older drama must have been a weakling.
Only lovers, then, dared to laugh at locksmiths. But
now locksmiths sit brooding on the past, shriveled to
mean uses, ready for paltry kitchen jobs.

And the undertaker, what shall we say of him?
That black coat with the flower! That mournful
smile! That perfect grief! And yet, I am told,
undertakers, after hours, go singing home to supper,
and spend their evenings at the movies like us rougher
folk. It was David Copperfield, you recall, who
dined with an undertaker and his family—in the

room, no doubt, next to the coffin storage—and he remarked at the time how cheerfully the joint went round. One of this sober cloth, moreover, has confided to me that they let themselves loose, above all professions, in their reunions and conventions. If an unusual riot issues from the door and a gay fellow goes walking on the table it is sure that either lawyers or undertakers sit inside.

For myself, if I were to become a merchant, I would choose a shop at a four-corners in the country, and I would stock from shoe-laces to plows. There is no virtue in keeping store in the city. It is merely by favor that customers show themselves. Candidly, your competitor can better supply their wants. This is not so at the four-corners. Nor is anyone a more influential citizen than a country merchant. He sets the style in calicoes. He judges between check and stripe. His decision against a high heel flattens the housewives by an inch. But if I kept such a country store, I would provide an open fire and, when the shadows lengthened, an easy chair or two for gossips.

I was meditating lately on these strange preferences in livelihoods and was gazing through the city windows for any clue when I was reminded of a tempting scheme that Wee Jessie—a delightful Scotswoman of my acquaintance—has planned for several of us.

We are to be traveling merchants for a season, with a horse and wagon or a motor. My own preference is a motor, and already I see a vehicle painted in bright colors and opening up behind as spacious as a waffle cart. There will be windows all around for the display of goods. It is not quite fixed what we shall sell. Wee Jessie leans toward bonnets and little millinery odds and ends. I am for kitchen tins. M—— inclines toward drygoods, serviceable fabrics. It is thought that we shall live on the roof while on tour, with a canvas to draw on wet nights. We shall possess a horn—on which Wee Jessie once practiced in her youth—to gather up the crowd when we enter a village.

Fancy us, therefore, my dear sir, as taking the road late this coming spring in time to spread the summer's fashions. And if you hear our horn at twilight in your village—a tune of more wind than melody, unless Jessie shall cure her imperfections— know that on the morrow, by the pump, we shall display our wares.

The Tread of the Friendly Giants.

When our Babe he goeth walking in his garden,
Around his tinkling feet the sunbeams play.

IT has been my fortune to pass a few days where
there lives a dear little boy of less than three.
My first knowledge of him every morning is the
smothered scuffling through the partition as he
reluctantly splashes in his bath. Here, unless he
mend his caution, I fear he will never learn to play
the porpoise at the Zoo. Then there is a wee tapping
at my door. It is a fairy sound as though Mustard-
seed were in the hall. Or it might be Pease-blossom
rousing up Cobweb in the play, to repel the red-
hipped humble-bee. It is so slight a tapping that
if I sleep with even one ear inside the covers I will
not hear it.

The little lad stands in the dim passage to greet
me, fully dressed, to reproach me with my tardiness.

He is a mite of a fellow, but he is as wide awake and
shiny as though he were a part of the morning and
had been wrought delicately out of the dawn's first
ray. Indeed, I choose to fancy that the sun, being
off hurriedly on broader business, has made him his
agent for the premises. Particularly he assists in this
passage at my bedroom door where the sleepy Night,
which has not yet caught the summons, still stretches
and nods beyond the turn. It is so dark here on a
winter's morning when the nursery door is shut that
even an adventuring sunlight, if it chanced to clamber
through the window, would blink and falter in the
hazard of these turns. But the sun has sent a substitute better than himself: for is there not a shaft
of light along the floor? It can hardly fall from the
window or anywhere from the outside world.

The little lad stands in the passage demanding that
I get up. "Get up, lazybones!" he says. Pretty
language to his elders! He speaks soberly, halting
on each syllable of the long and difficult word. He
is so solemn that the jest is doubled. And now he
runs off, jouncing and stiff-legged to his nursery.
I hear him dragging his animals from his ark, telling
them all that they are lazybones, even his barking
dog and roaring lion. Noah, when he saw on that
first morning that his ark was grounded on Ararat,
did not rouse his beasts so early to leave the ship.

Later I meet the lad at breakfast, locked in his
high chair. In these riper hours of day there is less

of Cobweb in his composition. He is now every inch
a boy. He raps his spoon upon his tray. He hurls
food in the general direction of his mouth. If an
ear escape the assault it is gunnery beyond the
common. He is bibbed against misadventure. This
morning he yearns loudly for muffins, which he calls
"bums." He chooses those that are unusually brown
with a smudge of the cooking-tin, and these he calls
"dirty bums."

Such is my nephew—a round-cheeked, blue-eyed
rogue who takes my thumb in all his fingers when
we go walking. His jumpers are slack behind and
they wag from side to side in an inexpressibly funny
manner, but this I am led to believe springs not from
any special genius but is common to all children.
It is only recently that he learned to walk, for although he was forward with his teeth and their early
sprouting ran in gossip up the street, yet he lagged
in locomotion. Previously he advanced most surely
on his seat—his slider, as he called it—throwing out
his legs and curling them in under so as to draw him
after. By this means he attained a fine speed upon
a slippery floor, but he chafed upon a carpet. His
mother and I agreed that this was quite an unusual
method and that it presaged some rare talent for his
future, as the scorn of a rattle is said to predict a
judge. It was during one of these advances across
the kitchen floor where the boards are rough that an
accident occurred. As he excitedly put it, with a

fitting gesture to the rear, he got a sliver in his slider. But now he goes upon his feet with a waddle like a sailor, and he wags his slider from side to side.

Sometimes we play at hide-and-seek and we pop out at one another from behind the sofa. He lacks ingenuity in this, for he always hides in the same place. I have tempted him for variety to stow himself in the woodbox. Or the pantry would hold him if he squeezed in among the brooms. Nor does my ingenuity surpass his, for regularly in a certain order I shake the curtains at the door and spy under the table. I stir the wastebasket and peer within the vases, although they would hardly hold his shoe. Then when he is red-hot to be found and is already peeking impatiently around the sofa, at last I cry out his discovery and we begin all over again.

I play ball with him and bounce it off his head, a game of more mirth in the acting than in the telling. Or we squeeze his animals for the noises that they make. His lion in particular roars as though lungs were its only tenant. But chiefly I am fast in his friendship because I ride upon his bear. I take the door at a gallop. I rear at the turn. I fall off in my most comical fashion. Sometimes I manage to kick over his blocks; at which we call it a game, and begin again. He has named the bear in my honor.

We start all of our games again just as soon as we have finished them. That is what a game is. And if it is worth playing at all, it is worth endless repetition.

If I strike a rich deep tone upon the Burmese gong, I must continue to strike upon it until I can draw his attention to something else. Once, the cook, hearing the din, thought that I hinted for my dinner. Being an obliging creature, she fell into such a flurry and so stirred her pans to push the cooking forward, that presently she burned the meat.

Or if I moo like a cow, I must moo until sunset. I rolled off the sofa once to distract him when the ugly world was too much with him. Immediately he brightened from his complaint and demanded that I do it once more. And lately, when a puppy bounced out of the house next door and, losing its footing, rolled heels over head to the bottom of the steps, at once he pleaded for an encore. To him all the world's a stage.

My nephew observes me closely to see what kind of fellow I am. I study him, too. He watches me over the top of his mug at breakfast and I stare back at him over my coffee cup. If I wrinkle my nose, he wrinkles his. If I stick out my tongue, he sticks his out, too. He answers wink with wink. When I pet his woolly lamb, however, he seems to wonder at my absurdity. When I wind up his steam engine, certainly he suspects that I am a novice. He shows a disregard of my castles, and although I build them on the windy vantage of a chair, with dizzy battlements topping all the country, he brushes them into ruin.

Sometimes I fancy that his glance is mixed with scorn, and that he considers my attempts to amuse him as rather a silly business. I wonder what he thinks about when he looks at me seriously. I cannot doubt his wisdom. He seems to resemble a philosopher who has traveled to us from a distant world. If he cast me a sentence from Plato, I would say, "Master, I listen." Is it Greek he speaks, or a dark language from a corner of the sky? He has a far-off look as though he saw quite through these superficial affairs of earth. His eyes have borrowed the color of his wanderings and they are as blue as the depths beyond the moon. And I think of another child, somewhat older than himself, whose tin soldiers these many years are rusted, a thoughtful silent child who was asked, once upon a time, what he did when he got to bed. "Gampaw," he replied, "I lies and lies, Gampaw, and links and links, 'til I know mos' everysin'." The snow of a few winters, the sun of summer, the revolving stars and seasons—until this lad now serves in France.

My nephew, although he too roams these distant spaces of philosophic thought and brings back strange unexpected treasure, has not arrived at the age of mere terrestrial exploration. He is quite ignorant of his own house and has no curiosity about the back stairs—the back stairs that go winding darkly from the safety of the kitchen. Scarcely is the fizzing of dinner lost than a new strange world engulfs one.

He is too young to know that a doorway in the dark is the portal of adventure. He does not know the mystery and the twistings of the cellar, or the shadows of the upper hallway and the dim hollows that grow and spread across the twilight.

Dear lad, there is a sunny world beyond the garden gate, cities and rolling hills and far-off rivers with white sails going up and down. There are wide oceans, and ships with tossing lights, and islands set with palm trees. And there are stars above your roof for you to wonder at. But also, nearer home, there are gentle shadows on the stairs, a dim cellar for the friendly creatures of your fancy, and for your exalted mood there is a garret with dark corners. Here, on a braver morning, you may push behind the trunks and boxes and come to a land unutterable where the furthest Crusoe has scarcely ventured. Or in a more familiar hour you may sit alongside a window high above the town. Here you will see the milkman on his rounds with his pails and long tin dipper. And these misty kingdoms that open so broadly on the world are near at hand. They are yours if you dare to go adventuring for them.

Soon your ambition will leap its nursery barriers. No longer will you be content to sit inside this quiet room and pile your blocks upon the floor. You will be off on discovery of the long trail that lies along the back hall and the pantry where the ways are dark. You will wander in search of the caverns that lie

beneath the stairs when the night has come. You
will trudge up steps and down for any lurking ocean
on which to sail your pirate ships. Already I see you
gazing with wistful eyes into the spaces beyond the
door—into the days of your great adventure. In
your thought is the patter and scurry of new crea-
tion. It is almost fairy time for you. The tread of
the friendly giants, still far off, is sounding in the
dark. . . .

Dear little lad, in this darkness may there be no
fear! For these shadows of the twilight—which too
long have been chased like common miscreants with
lamp and candle—are really friendly beings and they
wait to romp with you. Because thieves have walked
in darkness, shall darkness be called a thief? Rather,
let the dark hours take their repute from the countless gracious spirits that are abroad—the quieter
fancies that flourish when the light has gone—the
gentle creatures that leave their hiding when the sun
has set. When a rug lies roughened at close of day,
it is said truly that a fairy peeps from under to learn
if at last the house is safe. And they hide in the
hallway for the signal of your coming, yet so timid
that if the fire is stirred they scamper beyond the
turn. They huddle close beneath the stairs that they
may listen to your voice. They come and go on tiptoe when the curtain sways, in the hope that you will
follow. With their long thin shadowy fingers they
beckon for you beneath the sofa.

The time is coming when you can no longer resist their invitation, when you will leave your woolly lamb and your roaring lion on this dull safe hearth and will go on pilgrimage. The back stairs sit patient in the dark for your hand upon the door. The great dim garret that has sat nodding for so many years will smile at last at your coming. It has been lonely so long for the glad sound of running feet and laughter. It has been childless so many years.

But once children's feet played there and romped through the short winter afternoons. A rope hung from post to post and furnished forth a circus. Here giant swings were hazarded. Here children hung from the knees until their marbles and other wealth dropped from their pockets. And for less ambitious moments there were toys—

> The little toy dog is covered with dust,
> But sturdy and stanch he stands;
> And the little toy soldier is red with rust,
> And his musket moulds in his hands.
> Time was when the little toy dog was new,
> And the soldier was passing fair;
> And that was the time when our Little Boy Blue
> Kissed them and put them there.

And now Little Boy Blue again climbs the long stairs. He stretches up on tiptoe to turn the door-knob at the top. He listens as a prudent explorer should. Cook rattles her tins below, but it is a far-off sound as from another world. Somewhere, doubtless, the friendly milkman's bell goes jingling up the street. There is a distant barking of familiar dogs. Will it not be better to return to the safe regions and watch the traffic from the window? But here, beckoning, is the great adventure.

The brave die is cast. He advances with outstretched arms into the darkness. Suddenly, behind him, the door swings shut. The sound of cooking-tins is lost. Silence. Silence, except for branches scratching on the roof. But the garret hears the sound of feet, and it rouses itself and rubs its dusky eyes.

But when darkness thickens and the sunlight has vanished from the floor, then comes the magic hour. The garret then tears from its eyes the blind bandage of the day. Strange creatures lift their heads. And now, as you wait expectant, there comes a mysterious sound from the darkest corner. Is it a mouse that stirs? Rather, it seems a far-off sound, as though a blind man, tapping with his stick, walked on the margin of the world. The noise comes near. It gains in volume. It is close at hand. Dear lad, you have come upon the magic hour. It is the tread of the friendly giants that is sounding in the dark. . . .

On Spending a Holiday.

AT a party lately a worn subject came under discussion.

Our host lives in a triangular stone-paved courtyard tucked off from the thoroughfare but with the rattle of the elevated railway close at hand. The building is of decent brick, three stories in height, and it exhibits to the courtyard a row of identical doorsteps. The entrance to the courtyard is a swinging shutter between buildings facing on the street, and it might seem a mystery—like the apple in the dumpling—how the building inside squeezed through so narrow an entrance. Yet here it is, with a rubber plant in one corner and a trellis for imaginary vines in the other.

In this courtyard, *Pomander Walk* might be acted along the stoops. For a necessary stage property—you recall, of course, the lamplighter with his ladder in the second act!—there is a gas lamp of old design in the middle of the enclosure, up near the footlights, as it were. From the stoops the main comedy might proceed, with certain business at the upper windows—the profane Admiral with the timber leg popping his head out of one, the mysterious fat man—in some sort the villain of the piece—putting his head out of another to woo the buxom

widow at a third. And then the muffin man! In
the twilight when the lamp is lighted and the heroine
at last is in the hero's arms, there would be a pleasant
crunching of muffins at all the windows as the curtain
falls.

But I shall not drop even a hint as to the location
of this courtyard. Many persons think that New
York City is but a massive gridiron, and they are
ignorant of the nooks and quirks and angles of the
lower town. Enough that the Indian of a modest
tobacconist guards the swinging shutter of the entrance to the courtyard.

Here we sat in the very window I had designed for
the profane Admiral, and talked in the quiet interval
between trains.

One of our company—a man whom I shall call
Flint—was hardy enough to say that he never employed his leisure in going to the country—that a
walk about the city streets was his best refreshment.
Flint's livelihood is cotton. He is a dumpish sort
of person who looks as if he needed exercise, but he
has a sharp clear eye. At first his remark fell on us
as a mere perversity, as of one who proclaims a
humorous whim. And yet he adhered tenaciously
to his opinion, urging smooth pavements against
mud, the study of countless faces against the song of
birds and great buildings against cliffs.

Another of our company opposed him in this—
Colum, who chafes as an accountant. Colum is a

gentle dreamy fellow who likes birds. All winter he
saves his tobacco tins which, in his two weeks' vacation in the country, he sets up in trees as birdhouses.
He confesses that he took up with a certain brand
of tobacco because its receptacle is popular with
wrens. Also he cultivated a taste for waffles—which
at first by a sad distortion of nature he lacked—for
no other reason except that syrup may be bought in
pretty log-cabin tins particularly suited for bluebirds.
If you chance to breakfast with him, he urges the
syrup on you with pleasant and insistent hospitality.
With satisfaction he drains a can. By June he has
a dozen of these empty cabins on the shelf alongside
his country boots. Time was when he was lean of
girth—as becomes an accountant, who is hinged
dyspeptically all day across his desk—but by this
agreeable stowage he has now grown to plumpness.
When in the country Colum rises early in order to
stretch the pleasures of the day, and he walks about
before breakfast from tree to tree to view his feath-
ered tenants. He has even acquired, after much
practice, the knack of chirping—a hissing conjunc-
tion of the lips and teeth—which he is confident wins
the friendly attention of the birds.

Flint heard Colum impatiently, and interrupted
before he was done. "Pooh!" he said. "There's mud
in the country, and not much of any plumbing, and
in the morning it's cold until you light a fire."

"Of course," said Colum. "But I love it. Perhaps

you remember, Flint, the old willow stump out near the road. I put a Barking Dog on top of it, and now there's a family of wrens inside."

"Nonsense," said Flint. "There is too much climate in the country—much more than in town. It's either too hot or too cold. And it's lonely. As for you, Colum, you're sentimental about your bird-houses. And you dislike your job. You like the country merely because it is a symbol of a holiday. It is freedom from an irksome task. It means a closing of your desk. But if you had to live in the country, you would grumble in a month's time. Even a bullfrog—and he is brought up to it, poor wretch—croaks at night."

Colum interrupted. "That's not true, Flint. I know I'd like it—to live on a farm and keep chickens. Sometimes in winter, or more often in spring, I can hardly wait for summer and my two weeks. I look out of the window and I see a mirage—trees and hills." Colum sighed. "It's quite wonderful, that view, but it unsettles me for my ledger."

"That's it," broke in Flint. "Your sentimentality spoils your happiness. You let two weeks poison the other fifty. It's immoral."

Colum was about to retort, when he was anticipated by a new speaker. It was Quill, the journalist, who has long thin fingers and indigestion. At meals he pecks suspiciously at his plate, and he eats food substitutes. Quill runs a financial supplement, or something of that kind, to a daily paper. He always knows whether Steel is strong and whether Copper is up or down. If you call on him at his office, he glances at you for a moment before he knows you. Yet in his slippers he grows human.

"I like the country, too," he interposed, "and no one ever said that I am sentimental." He tapped his head. "I'm as hard as nails up here." Quill cracked his knuckles in a disagreeable habit he has, and continued: "I have a shack on the West Shore, and I go there week-ends. My work is so confining that if I didn't get to the country once in a while, I would play out in a jiffy. I'm a nervous frazzle—a nervous frazzle—by Saturday noon. But I lie on the grass all Sunday, and if nobody snaps at me and I am let alone, by Monday morning I am fit again."

"You must be like Antæus."

This remark came from Wurm, our host. Wurm is a bookish fellow who wears great rimmed glasses. He spends much of his time in company thinking up apposite quotations and verifying them. He has worn out two Bartlett's. Wurm is also addicted to maps and dictionaries, and is a great reader of special articles. Consequently his mind is a pound for stray collarless facts; or rather, in its variety of contents, it more closely resembles a building contractor's back yard—odd salvage—rejected doors—a job of window-frames—a pile of bricks for chipping—discarded plumbing—broken junk gathered here and there. Mr. Aust himself, a building contractor who once lived on our street—a man of no broad fame— quite local—surely unknown to you—did not collect so wide a rubbish.

However, despite these qualities, Wurm is rather a pleasant and harmless bit of cobweb. For a liveli- hood, he sits in a bank behind a grill. At noon he eats his lunch in his cage, and afterwards with a rubber band he snaps at the flies. In the hunting season he kills in a day as many as a dozen of these pests and ranges them in his pen tray. On Saturday afternoon he rummages in Malkan's and the second- hand bookshops along Fourth Avenue. To see Wurm in his most characteristic pose, is to see him on a ladder, with one leg outstretched, far off his bal- ance, fumbling for a title with his finger tips. Surely, in these dull alcoves, gravity nods on its job. Then he buys a sour red apple at the corner and pelts home to dinner. This is served him on a tin tray by his stout landlady who comes puffing up the stairs. It is a bit of pleasant comedy that whatever dish is served happens to be the very one of which he was thinking as he came out of the bank. By this inno- cent device he is popular with his landlady and she skims the milk for him.

Wurm rapped his pipe bowl on the arm of his chair. "You must be like Antæus," he replied.

"Like what?" asked Flint.

"Antæus—the fellow who wrestled with Hercules. Each time that Antæus was thrown against the earth his strength was doubled. He was finally in the way of overcoming Hercules, when Hercules by seizing him around the middle lifted him off the ground. By this strategy he deprived him of all contact with the earth, and presently Antæus weakened and was vanquished."

"That's me," said Quill, the journalist. "If I can't get back to my shack on Sunday, I feel that Hercules has me, too, around the middle."

"Perhaps I can find the story," said Wurm, his eye running toward the bookshelves.

"Don't bother," said Flint.

There was now another speaker—Flannel Shirt, as we called him—who had once been sated with formal dinners and society, and is now inclined to cry them down. He leans a bit toward socialism and free verse. He was about to praise the country for its freedom from sordidness and artificiality, when Flint, who had heard him before, interrupted.

"Rubbish!" he cried out. "All of you, but in different ways, are slaves to an old tradition kept up by Wordsworth, who would himself, doubtless, have moved to London except for the steepness of the rents. You all maintain that you like the country, yet on one excuse or another you live in the city and growl about it. There isn't a commuter among you. Honest folk, these commuters, with marrow in their bones—a steak in a paper bag—the sleet in their faces

on the ferryboat.   I am the only one who admits that
he lives in the city because he prefers it.   The country
is good enough to read about—I like it in books—
but I choose to sit meantime with my feet on a city
fender."

Here Wurm broke in again.   "I see, Flint," he
said, "that you have been reading Leslie Stephen."

Flint denied it.

"Well, anyway, you have quoted him.   Let me
read you a bit of his essay on 'Country Books.' "

Flint made a grimace.   "Wurm always has a
favorite passage."

Wurm went to a shelf and took down a volume.
He blew off the dust and smoothed its sides.
"Listen to this!" he said.   "Picked up the volume at
Schulte's, on the twenty-five cent table.   'A love of
the country is taken,' " he read, " 'I know not why,
to indicate the presence of all the cardinal vir-
tues. . . . We assert a taste for sweet and innocent
pleasures and an indifference to the feverish excite-
ments of artificial society.   I, too, like the country, . . .' (you'll like this, Flint) 'but I confess—to
be duly modest—that I love it best in books.   In real
life I have remarked that it is frequently damp and
rheumatic, and most hated by those who know it
best. . . . Though a cockney in grain, I love to lean
upon the farmyard gate; to hear Mrs. Poyser give
a bit of her mind to the squire; to be lulled into a
placid doze by the humming of Dorlecote Mill; to sit

down in Dandie Dinmont's parlour . . . or to drop into the kitchen of a good old country inn, and to smoke a pipe with Tom Jones or listen to the simple-minded philosophy of Parson Adams.' "

"You hit on a good one then," said Flint. "And now as I was saying—"

Wurm interposed. "Just a moment, Flint! You think that that quotation supports your side of the discussion. Not at all. It shows merely that sometimes we get greater reality from books than we get from life. Leslie Stephen liked the real country, also. In his holidays he climbed the Swiss mountains—wrote a book about them—it's on that top shelf. Don't you remember how he loved to roll stones off a cliff? And as a pedestrian he was almost as famous as George Borrow—walked the shirt off his back before his college trustees and all that sort of thing. But he got an even sharper reality from books. He liked the city, too, but in many a mood, there's no doubt about it, he preferred to walk to Charing Cross with Doctor Johnson in a book, rather than to jostle on the actual pavement outside his door."

"Speed up, Wurm!" This from Quill, the journalist. "Inch along, old caterpillar!"

"As far as I am concerned," Wurm continued, "I would rather go with Charles and Mary Lamb to see *The Battle of Hexham* in their gallery than to any show in Times Square. I love to think of that fine old pair climbing up the stairs, carefully at the turn, lest they tread on a neighbor's heels. Then the pleasant gallery, with its great lantern to light their expectant faces!"

Wurm's eyes strayed again wistfully to his shelves. Flint stayed him. "And so you think that it is possible to see life completely in a mirror."

"By no means," Wurm returned. "We must see it both ways. Nor am I, as you infer, in any sense like the Lady of Shalott. A great book cannot be compared to a mirror. There is no genius in a mirror. It merely reflects the actual, and slightly darkened. A great book shows life through the medium of an individuality. The actual has been lifted into truth. Divinity has passed into it through the unobstructed channel of genius."

Here Flint broke in. "Divinity—genius—the Swiss Alps—*The Battle of Hexham*—what have they to do with Quill's shack out in Jersey or Colum's dirty birdhouses? You jump the track, Wurm. When everybody is heading for the main tent, you keep running to the side-shows."

Quill, the journalist, joined the banter. "You remind me, Wurm—I hate to say it—of what a sea captain once said to me when I tried to loan him a book. 'Readin',' he said, 'readin' rots the mind.' "

It was Colum's turn to ask a question. "What do *you* do, Flint," he asked, "when you have a holiday?"

"Me? Well, I don't run off to the country as if

the city were afire and my coat-tails smoked. And
I don't sentimentalize on the evils of society. And
I don't sit and blink in the dark, and moon around
on a shelf and wear out books. I go outdoors. I
walk around and look at things—shop windows and
all that, when the merchants leave their curtains up.
I walk across the bridges and spit off. Then there's
the Bronx and the Battery, with benches where one
may make acquaintances. People are always more
communicative when they look out on the water.
The last time I sat there an old fellow told me about
himself, his wife, his victrola and his saloon. I talk
to a good many persons, first and last, or I stand
around until they talk to me. So many persons wear
blinders in the city. They don't know how wonderful
it is. Once, on Christmas Eve, I pretended to shop
on Fourteenth Street, just to listen to the crowd on
its final round—mother's carpet sweeper, you understand, or a drum for the heir. A crowd on Christmas
is different—it's gayer—reckless—it's an exalted
Saturday night. Afterwards I heard Midnight Mass
at the Russian Cathedral. Then there are always
ferryboats—the band on the boat to Staten Island—
God! What music! Tugs and lights. I would like
to know a tug—intimately. If more people were
like tugs we'd have less rotten politics. Wall Street
on a holiday is fascinating. No one about. Desolate.
But full of spirits."

Flint took a fresh cigar. "Last Sunday morning

I walked in Central Park. There were all manner
of toy sailboats on the pond—big and little—thirty
of them at the least—tipping and running in the
breeze. Grown men sail them. They set them on a
course, and then they trot around the pond and wait
for them. Presently I was curious. A man upward
of fifty had his boat out on the grass and was adjust-
ing the rigging.

" 'That's quite a boat,' I began.

" 'It's not a bad tub,' he answered.

" 'Do you hire it from the park department?' I
asked.

" 'No!' with some scorn.

" 'Where do you buy them?'

" 'We don't buy them.'

" 'Then how—?' I started.

" 'We make 'em—nights.'

"He resumed his work. The boat was accurately
and beautifully turned—hollow inside—with a deck
of glossy wood. The rudder was controlled by finest
tackle and hardware. Altogether, it was as delicately
wrought as a violin.

" 'It's this way!'—its builder and skipper laid
down his pipe—'There are about thirty of us boys
who are dippy about boats. We can't afford real
boats, so we make these little ones. Daytimes I am
an interior decorator. This is a thirty-six. Next
winter—if my wife will stand the muss (My God!
How it litters up the dining-room!) I am going to

build a forty-two. All of the boys bring out a new boat each spring!' The old fellow squinted at his mast and tightened a cord. Then he continued. 'If you are interested, come around any Sunday morning until the pond is frozen. And if you want to try your hand at a boat this winter, just ask any of us boys and we will help you. Your first boat or two will be sad—*Ju - das!* But you will learn.'"

Flint was interrupted by Quill. "Isn't that rather a silly occupation for grown men?"

"It's not an occupation," said Flint. "It's an avocation, and it isn't silly. Any one of us would enjoy it, if he weren't so self-conscious. And it's more picturesque than golf and takes more skill. And what courtesy! These men form what is really a club—a club in its primitive and true sense. And I was invited to be one of them."

Flannel Shirt broke in. "By George, that *was* courtesy. If you had happened on a polo player at his club—a man not known to you—he wouldn't have invited you to come around and bring your pony for instruction."

"It's not an exact comparison, is it, Old Flannel Shirt?"

"No, maybe not."

There was a pause. It was Flint who resumed. "I rather like to think of that interior decorator littering up his dining-room every night—clamps and glue-pots on the sideboard—hardly room for the sugar-bowl—lumber underneath—and then bringing out a new boat in the spring."

Wurm looked up from the couch. "Stevenson," he said, "should have known that fellow. He would have found him a place among his Lantern Bearers."

Flint continued. "From the pond I walked down Fifth Avenue."

"It's Fifth Avenue," said Flannel Shirt, "everything up above Fifty-ninth Street—and what it stands for, that I want to get away from."

"Easy, Flannel Shirt," said Flint. "Fifth Avenue doesn't interest me much either. It's too lonely. Everybody is always away. The big stone buildings aren't homes: they are points of departure, as somebody called them. And they were built for kings and persons of spacious lives, but they have been sublet to smaller folk. Or does no one live inside? You never see a curtain stir. There is never a face at a window. Everything is stone and dead. One might think that a Gorgon had gone riding on a 'bus top, and had thrown his cold eye upon the house fronts." Flint paused. "How can one live obscurely, as these folk do, in the twilight, in so beautiful a shell? Even a crustacean sometimes shows his nose at his door. And yet what a wonderful street it would be if persons really lived there, and looked out of their windows, and sometimes, on clear days, hung their tapestries and rugs across the outer walls. Actually," added Flint, "I prefer to walk on the East Side. It is gayer."

"There is poverty, of course," he went on after a moment, "and suffering. But the streets are not depressing. They have fun on the East Side. There are so many children and there is no loneliness. If the street is blessed with a standpipe, it seems designed as a post for leaping. Any vacant wall—if the street is so lucky—serves for a game. There is baseball on the smooth pavement, or if one has a piece of chalk, he can lay out a kind of hopscotch—not stretched out, for there isn't room, but rolled up like a jelly cake. One must hop to the middle and out again. Or perhaps one is an artist and with a crayon he spends his grudge upon an enemy—these drawings can be no likeness of a friend. Or love guides the chalky fingers. And all the time slim-legged girls sit on curb and step and act as nursemaids to the younger fry."

"But, my word, what smells!"

"Yes, of course, and not very pleasant smells. Down on these streets we can learn what dogs think of us. But every Saturday night on Grand Street there is a market. I bought a tumbler of little nuts from an old woman. They aren't much good to eat— wee nuts, all shell—and they still sit in the kitchen getting dusty. It was raining when I bought them and the woman's hair was streaked in her face, but she didn't mind. There were pent roofs over all the carts.

Everything on God's earth was for sale. On the cart next to my old woman's, there was hardware— sieves, cullenders—kitchen stuff. And on the next, wearing gear, with women's stockings hung on a rope at the back. A girl came along carrying a pair of champagne-colored shoes, looking for stockings to match. Quite a belle. Somebody's girl. Quill, go down there on a Saturday night. It will make a column for your paper. I wonder if that girl found her stockings. A black-eyed Italian.

"But what I like best are the windows on the East Side. No one there ever says that his house is his castle. On the contrary it is his point of vantage— his outlook—his prospect. His house front never dozes. Windows are really windows, places to look out of—not openings for household exhibits—ornamental lamps or china things—at every window there is a head—somebody looking on the world. There is a pleasant gossip across the fire-escapes—a recipe for onions—a hint of fashion—a cure for rheumatism. The street bears the general life. The home is the street, not merely the crowded space within four walls. The street is the playground and the club— the common stage, and these are the galleries and boxes. We come again close to the beginning of the modern theatre—an innyard with windows round about. The play is shinny in the gutters. Venders come and go, selling fruit and red suspenders. An ice wagon clatters off, with a half-dozen children on its tailboard."

Flint flecked his ashes on the floor. "I wonder," he said at length, "that those persons who try to tempt these people out of the congested city to farms, don't see how falsely they go about it. They should reproduce the city in miniature—a dozen farmhouses must be huddled together to make a snug little town, where all the children may play and where the women, as they work, may talk across the windows. They must build villages like the farming towns of France.

"But where can one be so stirred as on the wharves? From here even the narrowest fancy reaches out to the four watery corners of the earth. No nose is so green and country-bred that it doesn't sniff the spices of India. Great ships lie in the channel camouflaged with war. If we could forget the terror of the submarine, would not these lines and stars and colors appear to us as symbols of the strange mystery of the far-off seas?

"Or if it is a day of sailing, there are a thousand barrels, oil maybe, ranged upon the wharf, standing at fat attention to go aboard. Except for numbers it might appear—although I am rusty at the legend— that in these barrels Ali Baba has hid his forty thieves for roguery when the ship is out to sea. Doubtless if one knocked upon a top and put his ear close upon a barrel, he would hear a villain's guttural voice inside, asking if the time were come.

"Then there are the theatres and parks, great caverns where a subway is being built. There are geraniums on window-sills, wash hanging on dizzy lines (cotton gymnasts practicing for a circus), a roar of traffic and shrill whistles, men and women eating— always eating. There has been nothing like this in all the ages. Babylon and Nineveh were only villages. Carthage was a crossroads. It is as though all the cities of antiquity had packed their bags and moved here to a common spot."

"Please, Flint," this from Colum, "but you forget that the faces of those who live in the country are happier. That's all that counts."

"Not happier—less alert, that's all—duller. For contentment, I'll wager against any farmhand the old woman who sells apples at the corner. She polishes them on her apron with—with spit. There is an Italian who peddles ice from a handcart on our street, and he never sees me without a grin. The folk who run our grocery, a man and his wife, seem happy all the day. No! we misjudge the city and we have done so since the days of Wordsworth. If we prized the city rightly, we would be at more pains to make it better—to lessen its suffering. We ought to go into the crowded parts with an eye not only for the poverty, but also with sympathy for its beauty—its love of sunshine—the tenderness with which the elder children guard the younger—its love of music—its dancing—its naturalness. If we had this sympathy we could help—*ourselves,* first—and after that, maybe, the East Side."

Flint arose and leaned against the chimney. He shook an accusing finger at the company. "You, Colum, ruin fifty weeks for the sake of two. You, Quill, hypnotize yourself into a frazzle by Saturday noon with unnecessary fret. You peck over your food too much. A little clear unmuddled thinking would straighten you out, even if you didn't let the ants crawl over you on Sunday afternoon. Old Flannel Shirt is blinded by his spleen against society. As for Wurm, he doesn't count. He's only a harmless bit of mummy-wrapping."

"And what are you, Flint?" asked Quill.

"Me? A rational man, I hope."

"You—you are an egotist. That's what you are."

"Very well," said Flint. "It's just as you say."

There was a red flash from the top of the Metropolitan Tower. Flint looked at his watch. "So?" he said, "I must be going."

And now that our party is over and I am home at last, I put out the light and draw open the curtains. Tomorrow—it is to be a holiday—I had planned to climb in the Highlands, for I, too, am addicted to the country. But perhaps—perhaps I'll change my plan and stay in town. I'll take a hint from Flint. I'll go down to Delancey Street and watch the chaffering and buying. What he said was true. He overstated his position, of course. Most propagandists do, being

swept off in the current of their swift conviction.
One should like both the city and the country; and
the liking for one should heighten the liking for the
other.   Any particular receptiveness must grow to
be a general receptiveness.   Yet, in the main, certainly, Flint was right.   I'll try Delancey Street, I
concluded, just this once.

Thousands of roofs lie below me, for I live in a
tower as of Teufelsdröckh.   And many of them
shield a bit of grief—darkened rooms where sick folk
lie—rooms where hope is faint.   And yet, as I believe,
under these roofs there is more joy than grief—more
contentment and happiness than despair, even in
these grievous times of war.   If Quill here frets himself into wakefulness and Colum chafes for the
coming of the summer, also let us remember that in
the murk and shadows of these rooms there are, at
the least, thirty sailors from Central Park—one old
fellow in particular who, although the hour is late,
still putters with his boat in the litter of his dining-
room.   Glue-pots on the sideboard!   Clamps among
the china, and lumber on the hearth!   And down on
Grand Street, snug abed, dreaming of pleasant con-
quest, sleeps the dark-eyed Italian girl.   On a chair
beside her are her champagne boots, with stockings
to match hung across the back.

Runaway Studies.

IN my edition of "Elia," illustrated by Brock, whose sympathetic pen, surely, was nibbed in days contemporary with Lamb, there is a sketch of a youth reclining on a window-seat with a book fallen open on his knees. He is clad in a long plain garment folded to his heels which carries a hint of a cathedral choir but which, doubtless, is the prescribed costume of an English public school. This lad is gazing through the casement into a sunny garden—for the artist's vague stippling invites the suspicion of grass and trees. Or rather, does not the intensity of his regard attest that his nimble thoughts have jumped the outmost wall? Already he journeys to those peaks and lofty towers that fringe the world of youth—a dizzy range that casts a magic border on his first wide thoughts, to be overleaped if he seek to tread the stars.

And yet it seems a sleepy afternoon. Flowers nod upon a shelf in the idle breeze from the open casement. On the warm sill a drowsy sunlight falls, as if the great round orb of day, having labored to the top of noon, now dawdled idly on the farther slope. A cat dozes with lazy comfort on the window-seat. Surely, this is the cat—if the old story be believed—the sleepiest of all her race, in whose dull ear the mouse dared to nest and breed.

This lad, who is so lost in thought, is none other than Charles Lamb, a mere stripling, not yet grown to his black small-clothes and sober gaiters, a shrill squeak of a boy scarcely done with his battledore. And here he sits, his cheek upon his palm, and dreams of the future.

But Lamb himself has written of this window-seat. Journeying northward out of London—in that wonderful middle age of his in which the Elia papers were composed—journeying northward he came once on the great country house where a part of his boyhood had been spent. It had been but lately given to the wreckers, "and the demolition of a few weeks," he writes, "had reduced it to—an antiquity."

"Had I seen those brick-and-mortar knaves at their process of destruction," he continues, "at the plucking of every pannel I should have felt the varlets at my heart. I should have cried out to them to spare a plank at least out of that cheerful store-room, in whose hot window-seat I used to sit and read Cowley, with the grass-plat before, and the hum and flappings of that one solitary wasp that ever haunted it about me—it is in mine ears now, as oft as summer returns. . . ."

I confess to a particular enjoyment of this essay, with its memory of tapestried bedrooms setting forth upon their walls "the unappeasable prudery of

Diana" under the peeping eye of Actæon; its echoing galleries once so dreadful when the night wind caught the candle at the turn; its hall of family portraits. But chiefly it is this window-seat that holds me—the casement looking on the garden and its southern sun-baked wall—the lad dreaming on his volume of Cowley, and leaping the garden border for the stars. These are the things that I admit most warmly to my affection.

It is not in the least that I am a lover of Cowley, who seems an unpleasantly antiquated author. I would choose, instead, that the youthful Elia were busy so early with one of his favorite Elizabethans. He has himself hinted that he read "The Vicar of Wakefield" in later days out of a tattered copy from a circulating library, yet I would willingly move the occasion forward, coincident to this. And I suspect that the artist Brock is also indifferent to Cowley: for has he not laid two other volumes handy on the shelf for the sure time when Cowley shall grow dull? Has he not even put Cowley flat down upon his face, as if, already neglected, he had slipped from the lad's negligent fingers—as if, indeed, Elia's far-striding meditation were to him of higher interest than the stiff measure of any poet?

I recall a child, dimly through the years, that lay upon the rug before the fire to read his book, with his chin resting on both his hands. His favorite hour was the winter twilight before the family came

together for their supper, for at that hour the lamplighter went his rounds and threw a golden string of
dots upon the street. He drove an old thin horse and
he stood on the seat of the cart with up-stretched
taper. But when the world grew dark the flare of
the fire was enough for the child to read, for he lay
close against the hearth. And as the shadows
gathered in the room, there was one story chiefly, of
such intensity that the excitement of it swept through
his body and out into his waving legs. Perhaps its
last copy has now vanished off the earth. It dealt
with a deserted house on a lonely road, where chains
clanked at midnight. Lights, too, seemingly not of
earth, glimmered at the windows, while groans—such
was the dark fancy of the author—issued from a
windy tower. But there was one supreme chapter
in which the hero was locked in a haunted room and
saw a candle at a chink of the wall. It belonged to
the villain, who nightly played there a ghostly antic
to frighten honest folk from a buried treasure.

And in summer the child read on the casement of
the dining-room with the window up. It was the
height of a tall man from the ground, and this gave
it a bit of dizziness that enhanced the pleasure. This
sill could be dully reached from inside, but the approach from the outside was riskiest and best. For
an adventuring mood this window was a kind of
postern to the house for innocent deception, beyond
the eye of both the sitting-room and cook. Some-

times it was the bridge of a lofty ship with a pilot
going up and down, or it was a lighthouse to mark a
channel. It was as versatile as the kitchen step-
ladder which—on Thursday afternoons when the
cook was out—unbent from its sober household duties
and joined him as an equal. But chiefly on this sill
the child read his books on summer days. His cousins
sat inside on chairs, starched for company, and read
safe and dimpled authors, but his were of a vagrant
kind. There was one book, especially, in which a lad
not much bigger than himself ran from home and
joined a circus. A scolding aunt was his excuse.
And the child on the sill chafed at his own happy
circumstance which denied him these adventures.

In a dark room in an upper story of the house
there was a great box where old books and periodicals
were stored. No place this side of Cimmeria had
deeper shadows. Not even the underground stall of
the neighbor's cow, which showed a gloomy window
on the garden, gave quite the chill. It was only on
the brightest days that the child dared to rummage
in this box. The top of it was high and it was blind
fumbling unless he stood upon a chair. Then he bent
over, jack-knife fashion, until the upper part of
him—all above the legs—disappeared. In the ob-
scurity—his head being gone—it must have seemed
that Solomon lived upon the premises and had carried
out his ugly threat in that old affair of the disputed
child. Then he lifted out the papers—in particular

a set of *Leslie's Weekly* with battle pictures of the
Civil War.   Once he discovered a tale of Jules
Verne—a journey to the center of the earth—and he
spread its chapters before the window in the dusty
light.

But the view was high across the houses of the city
to a range of hills where tall trees grew as a hedge
upon the world.   And it was the hours when his book
lay fallen that counted most, for then he built poems
in his fancy of ships at sea and far-off countries.

It is by a fine instinct that children thus neglect
their books, whether it be Cowley or Circus Dick.
When they seem most truant they are the closest
rapt.   A book at its best starts the thought and sends
it off as a happy vagrant.   It is the thought that runs
away across the margin that brings back the richest
treasure.

But all reading in childhood is not happy.   It
chanced that lately in the long vacation I explored
a country school for boys.   It stood on the shaded
street of a pretty New England village, so perched
on a hilltop that it looked over a wide stretch of lower
country.   There were many marks of a healthful out-
door life—a football field and tennis courts, broad
lawns and a prospect of distant woodland for a holiday excursion.   It was on the steps of one of the
buildings used for recitation that I found a tattered
dog-eared remnant of *The Merchant of Venice*.   So
much of its front was gone that at the very first

of it Shylock had advanced far into his unworthy schemes. Evidently the book, by its position at the corner of the steps, had been thrown out immediately at the close of the final class, as if already it had been endured too long.

In the stillness of the abandoned school I sat for an hour and read about the choosing of the caskets. The margins were filled with drawings—one possibly a likeness of the teacher. Once there was a figure in a skirt—straight, single lines for legs—*Jack's girl*—scrawled in evident derision of a neighbor student's amatory weakness. There were records of baseball scores. Railroads were drawn obliquely across the pages, bending about in order not to touch the words, with a rare tunnel where some word stood out too long. Here and there were stealthy games of tit-tat-toe, practiced, doubtless, behind the teacher's back. Everything showed boredom with the play. What mattered it which casket was selected! Let Shylock take his pound of flesh! Only let him whet his knife and be quick about it! All's one. It's at best a sad and sleepy story suited only for a winter's day. But now spring is here—spring that is the king of all the seasons.

A bee comes buzzing on the pane. It flies off in careless truantry. The clock ticks slowly like a lazy partner in the teacher's dull conspiracy. Outside stretches the green world with its trees and hills

and moving clouds. There is a river yonder with
swimming-holes. A dog barks on a distant road.

Presently the lad's book slips from his negligent
fingers. He places it face down upon the desk. It
lies disregarded like that volume of old Cowley one
hundred years ago. His eyes wander from the black-
board where the *Merchant's* dry lines are scanned and
marked.

In sooth, I know not why I am so sad.

And then . . . his thoughts have clambered
through the window. They have leaped across the
schoolyard wall. Still in his ears he hears the jogging
of the *Merchant*—but the sound grows dim. Like
that other lad of long ago, his thoughts have jumped
the hills. Already, with giddy stride, they are
journeying to the profound region of the stars.

On Turning Into Forty.

THE other day, without any bells or whistles, I slipped off from the thirties. I felt the same sleepiness that morning. There was no apparent shifting of the grade.

I am conscious, maybe, that my agility is not what it was fifteen years ago. I do not leap across the fences. But I am not yet comic. Yonder stout man waddles as if he were a precious bombard. He strains at his forward buttons. Unless he mend his appetite, his shoes will be lost below his waistcoat. Already their tops and hulls, like battered caravels, disappear beneath his fat horizon. With him I bear no fellowship. But although nature has not stuffed me with her sweets to this thick rotundity; alas, despite of tubes and bottles, no shadowy garden flourishes on my top—waving capillary grasses and a prim path between the bush. Rather, I bear a general parade and smooth pleasance open to the glimpses of the moon.

And so at last I have turned into the forties. I remember now how heedlessly I had remarked a small brisk clock ticking upon the shelf as it counted the seconds—paying out to me, as it were, for my pleasure and expense, the brief coinage of my life. I had heard, also, unmindful of the warning, a tall and solemn clock as I lay awake, marking regretfully the progress of the night. And I had been told that water runs always beneath the bridge, that the deepest roses fade, that Time's white beard keeps growing to his knee. These phrases of wisdom I had heard and others. But what mattered them to me when my long young life lay stretched before me? Nor did the revolving stars concern me—nor the moon, spring with its gaudy brush, nor gray-clad winter. Nor did I care how the wind blew the swift seasons across the earth. Let Time's horses gallop, I cried. Speed! The bewildering peaks of youth are forward. The inn for the night lies far across the mountains.

But the seconds were entered on the ledger. At last the gray penman has made his footing. The great page turns. I have passed out of the thirties.

I am not given to brooding on my age. It is only by checking the years on my fingers that I am able to reckon the time of my birth. In the election booth, under a hard eye, I fumble the years and invite suspicion. Eighteen hundred and seventy-eight, I think it was. But even this salient fact—this milepost on my eternity—I remember most quickly by the recollection of a jack-knife acquired on my tenth birthday. By way of celebration on that day, having selected the longest blade, I cut the date—1888—in the kitchen woodwork with rather a pretty flourish when the cook was out. The swift events that followed the discovery—the dear woman paddled me with a great spoon through the door—fastened the occurrence in my memory.

It was about the year of the jack-knife that there lived in our neighborhood a bad boy whose name was Elmer. I would have quite forgotten him except that I met him on the pavement a few weeks ago. He was the bully of our street—a towering rogue with red hair and one suspender. I remember a chronic bandage which he shifted from toe to toe. This lad was of larger speech than the rest of us and he could spit between his teeth. He used to snatch the caps of the younger boys and went off with our baseball across the fences. He was wrapped, too, in mystery, and it was rumored—softly from ear to ear—that once he had been arrested and taken to the station-house.

And yet here he was, after all these years, not a bearded brigand with a knife sticking from his boot, but a mild undersized man, hat in hand, smiling at me with pleasant cordiality. His red hair had faded to a harmless carrot. From an overtopping rascal he had dwindled to my shoulder. It was as strange and incomprehensible as if the broken middle-aged gentleman, my familiar neighbor across the street who nods all day upon his step, were pointed out to me as Captain Kidd retired. Can it be that all villains come at last to a slippered state? Does Dick Turpin of the King's highway now falter with crutch along a garden path? And Captain Singleton, now that his last victim has walked the plank—does he doze on a sunny bench beneath his pear tree? Is no blood or treasure left upon the earth? Do all rascals lose their teeth? "Good evening, Elmer," I said, "it has been a long time since we have met." And I left him agreeable and smiling.

No, certainly I do not brood upon my age. Except for a gift I forget my birthday. It is only by an effort that I can think of myself as running toward middle age. If I meet a stranger, usually, by a pleasant deception, I think myself the younger, and because of an old-fashioned deference for age I bow and scrape in the doorway for his passage.

Of course I admit a suckling to be my junior. A few days since I happened to dine at one of the Purple Pups of our Greenwich Village. At my table, which was slashed with yellow and blue in the fashion of these places, sat a youth of seventeen who engaged me in conversation. Plainly, even to my blindness, he was younger than myself. The milk was scarcely dry upon his mouth. He was, by his admission across the soup, a writer of plays and he had received already as many as three pleasant letters of rejection. He flared with youth. Strange gases and opinion burned in his speech. His breast pocket bulged with manuscript, for reading at a hint.

I was poking at my dumpling when he asked me if I were a socialist. No, I replied. Then perhaps I was an anarchist or a Bolshevist, he persisted.

N-no, I answered him, sadly and slowly, for I foresaw his scorn. He leaned forward across the table. Begging my pardon for an intrusion in my affairs, he asked me if I were not aware that the world was slipping away from me. God knows. Perhaps. I had come frisking to that restaurant. I left it broken and decrepit. The youngster had his manuscripts and his anarchy. He held the wriggling world by its futuristic tail. It was not my world, to be sure, but it was a gay world and daubed with color.

And yet, despite this humiliating encounter, I feel quite young. Something has passed before me that may be Time. The summers have come and gone. There is snow on the pavement where I remember rain. I see, if I choose, the long vista of the years, with diminishing figures, and tin soldiers at the start. Yet I doubt if I am growing older. To myself I seem younger than in my twenties. In the twenties we are quite commonly old. We bear the whole weight of society. The world has been waiting so long for us and our remedies. In the twenties we scorn old authority. We let Titian and Keats go drown themselves. We are skeptical in religion, and before our unrelenting iron throne immortality and all things of faith plead in vain. Although I can show still only a shabby inventory, certainly I would not exchange myself for that other self in the twenties. I have acquired in these last few years a less narrow sympathy and a belief that some of my colder reasons

may be wrong. Nor would I barter certain knacks
of thoughts—serious and humorous—for the renewed
ability to leap across a five-foot bar. I am less fearful
of the world and its accidents. I have less embarrassment before people. I am less moody. I tack and
veer less among my betters for some meaner profit.
Surely I am growing younger.

I seem to remember reading a story in which a
scientist devised a means of reversing the direction
of the earth. Perhaps an explosion of gases back-
fired against the east. Perhaps he built a monstrous
lever and contrived the moon to be his fulcrum. Anyway, here at last was the earth spinning backward in
its course—the spring preceding winter—the sun
rising in the west—one o'clock going before twelve—
soup trailing after nuts—the seed-time following
upon the harvest. And so it began to appear—so
ran the story—that human life, too, was reversed.
Persons came into the world as withered grandames
and as old gentlemen with gold-headed canes, and
then receded like crabs backward into their maturity,
then into their adolescence and babyhood. To return
from a protracted voyage was to find your younger
friends sunk into pinafores. But the story was really
too ridiculous.

But in these last few years no doubt I do grow
younger. The great camera of the Master rolls its
moving pictures backward. Perhaps I am only
thirty-eight now that the direction is reversed.

I wonder what you thought, my dear X——, when
we met recently at dinner. We had not seen one
another very often in these last few years. Our paths
have led apart and we have not been even at shouting
distance across the fields. It is needless to remind
you, I hope, that I once paid you marked attention.
It began when we were boy and girl. Our friends

talked, you will recall. You were then less than a
year younger than myself, although no doubt you
have since lost distance. What a long time I spent
upon my tie and collar—a stiff high collar that
almost touched my ears! Some other turn of fortune's wheel—circumstance—a shaft of moonlight
(we were young, my dear)—a white frock—your
acquiescence—who knows?

I jilted you once or twice for other girls—nothing
formal, of course—but only when you had jilted me
three or four times. We once rowed upon a river at
night. Did I take your hand, my dear? If I listen
now I can hear the water dripping from the oar.
There was darkness—and stars—and youth (yourself, white-armed, the symbol of its mystery). Yes,
perhaps I am older now.

Was it not Byron who wrote?

> I am ashes where once I was fire,
> And the soul in my bosom is dead;
> What I loved I now merely admire,
> And my heart is as gray as my head.

I cannot pretend ever to have had so fierce a passion,
but at least my fire still burns and with a cheery blaze.
But you will not know this love of mine—unless, of
course, you read this page—and even so, you can only
suspect that I write of you, because, my dear, to be
quite frank, I paid attention to several girls beside
yourself.

Yes, they say that I have come to the top of the hill and that henceforth the view is back across my shoulder. I am counseled that with a turn of the road I had best sit with my back to the horses, for the mountains are behind. A little while and the finer purple will be showing in the west. Yet a little while, they say, and the bewildering peaks of youth will be gray and cold.

Perhaps some of the greener pleasures are mine no longer. Certainly, last night I went to the Winter Garden, but left bored after the first act; and I had left sooner except for climbing across my neighbors. I suppose there are young popinjays who seriously affirm that Ziegfeld's Beauty Chorus is equal to the galaxy of loveliness that once pranced at Weber and Field's when we came down from college on Saturday night. At old Coster and Bial's there was once a marvelous beauty who swung from a trapeze above the audience and scandalously undressed herself down to the fifth encore and her stockings. And, really, are there plays now as exciting as the *Prisoner of Zenda,* with its great fight upon the stairs—three men dead and the tables overturned—Red Rudolph, in the end, bearing off the Princess? Heroes no longer wear cloak and sword and rescue noble ladies from castle towers.

And Welsh rabbit, that was once a passion and the high symbol of extravagance, in these days has lost its finest flavor. In vain do we shake the paprika can. Pop-beer and real beer, its manly cousin, have neither of them the old foaming tingle when you come off the water. Yes, already, I am told, I am on the long road that leads down to the quiet inn at the mountain foot. I am promised, to be sure, many wide prospects, pleasant sounds of wind and water, and friendly greetings by the way. There will be a stop here and there for refreshments, a pause at the turn where the world shows best, a tightening of the brake. Get up, Dobbin! Go 'long! And then, tired and nodding, at last, we shall leave the upland and enter the twilight where all roads end.

A pleasant picture, is it not—a grandfather in a cap—yourself, my dear sir, hugging your cold shins in the chimney corner? Is it not a brave end to a stirring business? Life, you say, is a journey up and down a hill—aspirations unattained and a mild regret, castles at dawn, a brisk wind for the noontide, and at night, at best, the lights of a little village, the stir of water on the stones, and silence.

Is this true? Or do we not reiterate a lie? I deny old age. It is a false belief, a bad philosophy dimming the eyes of generations. Men and women may wear caps, but not because of age. In each one's heart, if he permit, a child keeps house to the very end. If Welsh rabbit lose its flavor, is it a sign of decaying power? I have yet to know that a relish for Shakespeare declines, or the love of one's friends, or the love of truth and beauty. Youth does not view the loftiest peaks. It is at sunset that the tallest castles rise.

My dear sir—you of seventy or beyond—if no rim of mountains stretches up before you, it is not your age that denies you but the quality of your thought. It has been said of old that as a man thinks so he is, but who of us has learned the lesson?

The journey has neither a beginning nor an end. Now is eternity. Our birth is but a signpost on the road—our going hence, another post to mark transition and our progress. The oldest stars are brief lamps upon our way. We shall travel wisely if we see peaks and castles all the day, and hold our childhood in our hearts. Then, when at last the night has come, we shall plant our second post upon a windy height where it will be first to catch the dawn.

On the Difference Between Wit and Humor.

I AM not sure that I can draw an exact line between wit and humor. Perhaps the distinction is so subtle that only those persons can decide who have long white beards. But even an ignorant man, so long as he is clear of Bedlam, may have an opinion.

I am quite positive that of the two, humor is the more comfortable and more livable quality. Humorous persons, if their gift is genuine and not a mere shine upon the surface, are always agreeable

companions and they sit through the evening best.
They have pleasant mouths turned up at the corners.
To these corners the great Master of marionettes has
fixed the strings and he holds them in his nimblest
fingers to twitch them at the slightest jest. But the
mouth of a merely witty man is hard and sour until
the moment of its discharge. Nor is the flash from a
witty man always comforting, whereas a humorous
man radiates a general pleasure and is like another
candle in the room.

I admire wit, but I have no real liking for it. It
has been too often employed against me, whereas
humor is always an ally. It never points an imperti-
nent finger into my defects. Humorous persons do
not sit like explosives on a fuse. They are safe and
easy comrades. But a wit's tongue is as sharp as a
donkey driver's stick. I may gallop the faster for its
prodding, yet the touch behind is too persuasive for
any comfort.

Wit is a lean creature with sharp inquiring nose,
whereas humor has a kindly eye and comfortable
girth. Wit, if it be necessary, uses malice to score a
point—like a cat it is quick to jump—but humor
keeps the peace in an easy chair. Wit has a better
voice in a solo, but humor comes into the chorus best.
Wit is as sharp as a stroke of lightning, whereas
humor is diffuse like sunlight. Wit keeps the season's
fashions and is precise in the phrases and judgments
of the day, but humor is concerned with homely

eternal things. Wit wears silk, but humor in home-
spun endures the wind. Wit sets a snare, whereas
humor goes off whistling without a victim in its mind.
Wit is sharper company at table, but humor serves
better in mischance and in the rain. When it tumbles
wit is sour, but humor goes uncomplaining without
its dinner. Humor laughs at another's jest and holds
its sides, while wit sits wrapped in study for a lively
answer. But it is a workaday world in which we
live, where we get mud upon our boots and come
weary to the twilight—it is a world that grieves and
suffers from many wounds in these years of war: and
therefore as I think of my acquaintance, it is those
who are humorous in its best and truest meaning
rather than those who are witty who give the more
profitable companionship.

And then, also, there is wit that is not wit. As
someone has written:

> Nor ever noise for wit on me could pass,
> When thro' the braying I discern'd the ass.

I sat lately at dinner with a notoriously witty person (a really witty man) whom our hostess had
introduced to provide the entertainment. I had read
many of his reviews of books and plays, and while I
confess their wit and brilliancy, I had thought them
to be hard and intellectual and lacking in all that
broader base of humor which aims at truth. His
writing—catching the bad habit of the time—is too

ready to proclaim a paradox and to assert the unusual,
to throw aside in contempt the valuable haystack in
a fine search for a paltry needle. His reviews are
seldom right—as most of us see the right—but they
sparkle and hold one's interest for their perversity
and unexpected turns.

In conversation I found him much as I had found
him in his writing—although, strictly speaking, it was
not a conversation, which requires an interchange of
word and idea and is turn about. A conversation
should not be a market where one sells and another
buys. Rather, it should be a bargaining back and
forth, and each person should be both merchant and
buyer. My rubber plant for your victrola, each
offering what he has and seeking his deficiency. It
was my friend B—— who fairly put the case when
he said that he liked so much to talk that he was
willing to pay for his audience by listening in his turn.

But this was a speech and a lecture. He loosed on
us from the cold spigot of his intellect a steady flow
of literary allusion—a practice which he professes to
hold in scorn—and wit and epigram. He seemed
torn from the page of Meredith. He talked like ink.
I had believed before that only people in books could
talk as he did, and then only when their author had
blotted and scratched their performance for a seventh
time before he sent it to the printer. To me it was
an entirely new experience, for my usual acquaintances are good common honest daytime woollen folk

and they seldom average better than one bright thing
in an evening.

At first I feared that there might be a break in his
flow of speech which I should be obliged to fill.   Once,
when there was a slight pause—a truffle was engaging
him—I launched a frail remark; but it was swept off
at once in the renewed torrent.   And seriously it does
not seem fair.   If one speaker insists—to change the
figure—on laying all the cobbles of a conversation,
he should at least allow another to carry the tarpot
and fill in the chinks.   When the evening was over,
although I recalled two or three clever stories, which
I shall botch in the telling, I came away tired and
dissatisfied, my tongue dry with disuse.

Now I would not seek that kind of man as a companion with whom to be becalmed in a sailboat, and
I would not wish to go to the country with him, least
of all to the North Woods or any place outside of
civilization.   I am sure that he would sulk if he were
deprived of an audience.   He would be crotchety at
breakfast across his bacon.   Certainly for the woods
a humorous man is better company, for his humor
in mischance comforts both him and you.   A humorous man—and here lies the heart of the matter—
a humorous man has the high gift of regarding an
annoyance in the very stroke of it as another man
shall regard it when the annoyance is long past.   If
a humorous person falls out of a canoe he knows the

exquisite jest while his head is still bobbing in the cold water. A witty man, on the contrary, is sour until he is changed and dry: but in a week's time when company is about, he will make a comic story of it.

My friend A—— with whom I went once into the Canadian woods has genuine humor, and no one can be a more satisfactory comrade. I do not recall that he said many comic things, and at bottom he was serious as the best humorists are. But in him there was a kind of joy and exaltation that lasted throughout the day. If the duffle were piled too high and fell about his ears, if the dinner was burned or the tent blew down in a driving storm at night, he met these mishaps as though they were the very things he had come north to get, as though without them the trip would have lacked its spice. This is an easy philosophy in retrospect but hard when the wet canvas falls across you and the rain beats in. A—— laughed at the very moment of disaster as another man will laugh later in an easy chair. I see him now swinging his axe for firewood to dry ourselves when we were spilled in a rapids; and again, while pitching our tent on a sandy beach when another storm had drowned us. And there is a certain cry of his (dully, *Wow!* on paper) expressive to the initiated of all things gay, which could never issue from the mouth of a merely witty man.

Real humor is primarily human—or divine, to be

exact—and after that the fun may follow naturally
in its order. Not long ago I saw Louis Jouvet of
the French Company play Sir Andrew Ague-Cheek.
It was a most humorous performance of the part, and
the reason is that the actor made no primary effort
to be funny. It was the humanity of his playing,
making his audience love him first of all, that pro-
voked the comedy. His long thin legs were comical
and so was his drawling talk, but the very heart and
essence was this love he started in his audience. Poor
fellow! how delightfully he smoothed the feathers in
his hat! How he feared to fight the duel! It was
easy to love such a dear silly human fellow. A merely
witty player might have drawn as many laughs, but
there would not have been the catching at the heart.

As for books and the wit or humor of their pages,
it appears that wit fades, whereas humor lasts.
Humor uses permanent nutgalls. But is there any-
thing more melancholy than the wit of another
generation? In the first place, this wit is intertwined
with forgotten circumstance. It hangs on a fashion—
on the style of a coat. It arose from a forgotten bit
of gossip. In the play of words the sources of the
pun are lost. It is like a local jest in a narrow coterie,
barren to an outsider. Sydney Smith was the most
celebrated wit of his day, but he is dull reading now.
Blackwood's at its first issue was a witty daring sheet,
but for us the pages are stagnant. I suppose that no
one now laughs at the witticisms of Thomas Hood.

Where are the wits of yesteryear? Yet the humor of
Falstaff and Lamb and Fielding remains and is a
reminder to us that humor, to be real, must be
founded on humanity and on truth.

On Going to a Party.

ALTHOUGH I usually enjoy a party when I have arrived, I seldom anticipate it with pleasure. I remain sour until I have hung my hat. I suspect that my disorder is general and that if any group of formal diners could be caught in preparation midway between their tub and over-shoes, they would be found a peevish company who might be expected to snap at one another. Yet look now at their smiling faces! With what zest they crunch their food! How cheerfully they clatter on their plates! Who would suspect that yonder smiling fellow who strokes his silky chin was sullen when he fixed his tie; or that this pleasant babble comes out of mouths that lately sulked before their mirrors?

I am not sure from what cause my own crustiness

proceeds. I am of no essential unsociability. Nor is it wholly the masquerade of unaccustomed clothes. I am deft with a bow-knot and patient with my collar. It may be partly a perversity of sex, inasmuch as we men are sometimes "taken" by our women folk. But chiefly it comes from an unwillingness to pledge the future, lest on the very night my own hearth appear the better choice. Here we are, with legs stretched for comfort toward the fire—easy and unbuttoned. Let the rain beat on the glass! Let chimneys topple! Let the wind whistle to its shrill companions of the North! But although I am led growling and reluctant to my host's door—with stiffened paws, as it were, against the sill—I usually enjoy myself when I am once inside. To see me across the salad smiling at my pretty neighbor, no one would know how churlish I had been on the coming of the invitation.

I have attended my share of formal dinners. I have dined with the magnificent H——s and their Roman Senator has announced me at the door; although, when he asked my name in the hall, I thought at first in my ignorance that he gave me directions about my rubbers. No one has faced more forks and knives, or has apportioned his implements with nicer discrimination among the meats. Not once have I been forced to stir my after-dinner coffee with a soup spoon. And yet I look back on these grand occasions with contentment chiefly because they are past. I

am in whole agreement with Cleopatra when she
spoke slightingly of her salad days—surely a fashionable afternoon affair at a castle on the river Nile—
when, as she confessed, she was young and green in
judgment.

It is usually a pleasure to meet distinguished persons who, as a rule, are friendly folk who sit in peace
and comfort. But if they are lugged in and set up
stiffly at a formal dinner they are too much an
exhibition. In this circumstance they cannot be
natural and at their best. And then I wonder how
they endure our abject deference and flabby sur-
render to their opinions. Would it not destroy all
interest in a game of bowling if the wretched pins
fell down before the hit were made? It was lately
at a dinner that our hostess held in captivity three of
these celebrated lions. One of them was a famous
traveler who had taken a tiger by its bristling beard.
The second was a popular lecturer. The third was
in distemper and crouched quietly at her plate. The
first two are sharp and bright and they roared to
expectation. But I do not complain when lions take
possession of the cage, for it reduces the general
liability of talk, and a common man, if he be indus-
trious, may pluck his bird down to the bone in peace.

A formal reception is even worse than a dinner.
One stands around with stalled machinery. Good
stout legs, that can go at a trot all day, become now
weak and wabbly. One hurdles dispiritedly over

trailing skirts. One tries in conversation to think of
the name of a play he has just seen, but it escapes
him. It is, however, so nearly in his grasp, that it
prevents him from turning to another topic. Benson,
the essayist, also disliked formal receptions and he
quotes Prince Hal in their dispraise. "Prithee, Ned,"
says the Prince—and I fancy that he has just led a
thirsty Duchess to the punchbowl, and was now in
the very act of escaping while her face was buried in
the cup—"Prithee, Ned," he says, "come out of this
fat room, and lend me thy hand to laugh a little!"
And we can imagine these two enfranchised rogues,
easy at heart, making off later to their Eastcheap
tavern, and the passing of a friendly cup. But now,
alas, today, all of the rooms of the house are fat and
thick with people. There is a confusion of tongues
as when work on the tower of Babel was broken off.
There is no escape. If it were one's good luck to be
a waiter, one could at least console himself that it was
his livelihood.

The furniture has been removed from all the rooms
in order that more persons may be more uncomfort-
able. Or perhaps the chairs and tables, like rats in a
leaky ship, have scuttled off, as it were, now that
fashion has wrecked the home. A friend of mine,
J——, resents these entertainments. No sooner,
recently, did he come into such a bare apartment
where, in happier days his favorite chair had stood,
than he hinted to the guests that the furniture had

been sold to meet the expenses of the day. This sorry jest lasted him until, on whispering to a servant, he learned that the chairs had been stored in an upper hall. At this he proposed that the party reassemble above, where at least they might sit down and be comfortable. When I last saw J—— that evening he was sitting at the turn of the stairs behind an exotic shrubbery, where he had found a vagrant chair that had straggled behind the upper emigration.

The very envelope that contains a formal invitation bears a forbidding look. It is massive and costly to the eye. It is much larger than a letter, unless, perhaps, one carries on a correspondence with a giant from Brobdingnag. You turn it round and round with sad premonition. The very writing is coldly impersonal without the pinch of a more human hand. It practices a chill anonymity as if it contains a warrant for a hanging. At first you hope it may be merely an announcement from your tailor, inasmuch as commerce patterns its advertisements on these social forms. I am told that there was once a famous man—a distinguished novelist—who so disliked formal parties but was so timid at their rejection that he took refuge in the cellar whenever one of these forbidding documents arrived, until he could forge a plausible excuse; for he believed that these colder and more barren rooms quickened his invention. The story goes that once when he was in an unusually timid state he lacked the courage to break the seal and so spent an uneasy morning upon the tubs, to the inconvenience of the laundress who thought that he fretted upon the plot. At last, on tearing off the envelope, he found to his relief that it was only a notice for a display of haberdashery at a fashionable shop. In his gratitude at his escape he at once sought his desk and conferred a blushing heiress on his hero.

But perhaps there are persons of an opposite mind who welcome an invitation. Even the preliminary rummage delights them when their clothes are sent for pressing and their choice wavers among their plumage. For such persons the superscription on the envelope now seems written in the spacious hand of hospitality.

But of informal dinners and the meeting of friends we can all approve without reserve. I recall, once upon a time, four old gentlemen who met every week for whist. Three of them were of marked eccentricity. One of them, when the game was at its pitch, reached down to the rungs of his chair and hitched it first to one side and then to the other, mussing up the rugs. The second had the infirmity of nodding his head continuously. Even if he played a trivial three spot, he sat on the decision and wagged his beard up and down like a judge. The third sucked his teeth and thereby made hissing noises. Later in the evening there would be served buttermilk or cider, and the sober party would adjourn at the gate. But there were two young rascals who practiced these

eccentricities and after they had gone to bed, for the
exquisite humor of it, they nodded their heads, too,
and sucked their teeth with loud hissing noises.

No one entertains more pleasantly than the S——
family and no one is more informal. If you come on
the minute for your dinner, it is likely that none of
the family is about. After a search J—— is found
in a flannel shirt in his garden with a watering-can.
"Hello!" he says in surprise. "What time is it?
Have you come already for dinner?"

"For God's sake," you reply—for I assume you
to be of familiar and profane manners—"get up and
wash yourself! Don't you know that you are giving
a party?"

J—— affects to be indignant. "Who is giving this
party, anyway?" he asks. "If it's yours, you run it!"
And then he leads you to the house, where you abuse
each other agreeably as he dresses.

Once a year on Christmas Eve they give a general
party. This has been a custom for a number of years
and it is now an institution as fixed as the night itself.
Invitations are not issued. At most a rumor goes
abroad to the elect that nine o'clock is a proper time
to come, when the children, who have peeked for
Santa Claus up the chimney, have at last been put to
bed. There is a great wood fire in the sitting-room
and, by way of andirons, two soldiers of the Continen-
tal Army keep up their endless march across the
hearth. The fireplace is encircled by a line of leather

cushions that rest upon the floor, like a window-seat that has undergone amputation of all its legs.

But the center of the entertainment is a prodigious egg-nog that rises from the dining table. I do not know the composition of the drink, yet my nose is much at fault if it includes aught but eggs and whiskey. At the end of the table J—— stands with his mighty ladle. It is his jest each year—for always there is a fresh stranger who has not heard it—it is his jest that the drink would be fair and agreeable to the taste if it were not for the superfluity of eggs which dull the mixture.

No one, even of a sour prohibition, refuses his entreaty. My aunt, who speaks against the Demon, once appeared at the party. She came sniffing to the table. "Ought I to take it, John?" she asked.

"Mildest thing you ever drank," said John, and he ladled her out a cup.

My aunt smelled it suspiciously.

"It's eggs," said John.

"Eggs?" said my aunt, "What a funny smell they have!" She said this with a facial expression not unlike that of Little Red Ridinghood, when she first saw the old lady with the long nose and sharp eyes.

"Nothing bad, I hope," said John.

"N-no," said my aunt slowly, and she took a sip.

"Of course the eggs spoil it a little," said John.

"It's very good," said my aunt, as she took another sip.

Then she put down her glass, but only when it was empty. "John," she said, "you are a rogue. You would like to get me tipsy." And at this she moved out of danger. Little Red Ridinghood escaped the wolf as narrowly. But did Little Red Ridinghood escape? Dear me, how one forgets!

But in closing I must not fail to mention an old lady and gentleman, both beyond eighty, who have always attended these parties. They have met old age with such trust and cheerfulness, and they are so eager at a jest, that no one of all the gathering fits the occasion half so well. And to exchange a word with them is to feel a pleasant contact with all the gentleness and mirth that have lodged with them during the space of their eighty years. The old gentleman is an astronomer and until lately, when he moved to a newer quarter of the town, he had behind his house in a proper tower a telescope, through which he showed his friends the moon. But in these last few years his work has been entirely mathematical and his telescope has fallen into disorder. His work finds a quicker comment among scientists of foreign lands than on his own street.

It is likely that tonight he has been busy with the computation of the orbit of a distant star up to the very minute when his wife brought in his tie and collar. And then arm and arm they have set out for the party, where they will sit until the last guest has gone.

Alas, when the party comes this Christmas, only one of these old people will be present, for the other with a smile lately fell asleep.

On a Pair of Leather Suspenders.

NOT long since I paid a visit to New Haven before daylight of a winter morning. I had hoped that my sleeper from Washington might be late and I was encouraged in this by the trainman who said that the dear old thing commonly went through New Haven at breakfast time. But it was barely three o'clock when the porter plucked at me in my upper berth. He intruded, happily, on a dream in which the train came rocking across the comforter.

Three o'clock, if you approach it properly through the evening, is said to have its compensations. There are persons (with a hiccough) who pronounce it the shank of the evening, but as an hour of morning it has few apologists. It is the early bird that catches the worm; but this should merely set one thinking before he thrusts out a foot into the cold morning, whether he may justly consider himself a bird or a worm. If no glad twitter rises to his lips in these early hours, he had best stay unpecked inside his coverlet.

It is hard to realize that other two-legged creatures like myself are habitually awake at this hour. In a wakeful night I may have heard the whistles and the clank of far-off wheels, and I may have known dimly that work goes on; yet for the most part I have fancied that the world, like a river steamboat in a fog, is tied at night to its shore: or if it must go plunging on through space to keep a schedule, that here and there a light merely is set upon a tower to warn the planets.

A locomotive was straining at its buttons, and from the cab a smoky engineer looked down on me. A truck load of boxes rattled down the platform. Crates of affable familiar hens were off upon a journey, bragging of their families. Men with flaring tapers tapped at wheels. The waiting-room, too, kept, as it were, one eye open to the night. The coffee-urn steamed on the lunch counter, and sandwiches sat inside their glass domes and looked darkly on the world.

It was the hour when "the tired burglar seeks his bed." I had thought of dozing in a hotel chair until breakfast, but presently a flood appeared in the persons of three scrub women. The fountains of the great deep were opened and the waters prevailed.

It still lacked an hour or so of daylight. I remembered that there used to be a humble restaurant and kitchen on wheels—to the vulgar, a dog-wagon—up toward York Street. This wagon, once upon a time, had appeased our appetites when we had been late for chapel and Commons. As an institution it was so trite that once we made of it a fraternity play. I faintly remember a pledge to secrecy—sworn by the moon and the seven wandering stars—but nevertheless I shall divulge the plot. It was a burlesque tragedy in rhyme. Some eighteen years ago, it seems, Brabantio, the noble Venetian Senator, kept this same dog-wagon—he and his beautiful daughter Desdemona. Here came Othello, Iago and Cassio of the famous class of umpty-ump.

The scene of the drama opens with Brabantio flopping his dainties on the iron, chanting to himself a lyric in praise of their tender juices. Presently Othello enters and when Brabantio's back is turned he makes love to Desdemona—a handsome fellow, this Othello, with the manner of a hero and curled moustachios. Exit Othello to a nine o'clock, Ladd on Confusions. Now the rascal Iago enters—myself! with flowing tie. He hates Othello. He glowers like a villain and soliloquizes:

> In order that my vengeance I may plot
> Give me a dog, and give it to me hot!

That was the kind of play. Finally, Desdemona is
nearly smothered but is returned at last to Othello's
arms. Iago meets his deserts. He is condemned to
join Δ K E, a rival fraternity. But the warm
heart of Desdemona melts and she intercedes to save
him from this horrid end. In mercy—behind the
scenes—his head is chopped off. Then all of us,
heroines and villains, sat to a late hour around the
fire and told one another how the real stage thirsted
for us. We drank lemonade mostly but we sang of
beer—one song about

> Beer, beer, glorious beer!
> Fill yourself right up to here!

accompanied with a gesture several inches above the
head. As the verses progressed it was customary to
stand on chairs and to reach up on tiptoe to show the
increasing depth.

But the dog-wagon has now become a gilded unfamiliar thing, twice its former size and with stools
for a considerable company. I questioned the proprietor whether he might be descended from the noble
Brabantio, but the dull fellow gave no response. The
wagon has passed to meaner ownership.

Across the street Vanderbilt Hall loomed indis-
tinctly. To the ignorant it may be necessary to
explain that its courtyard is open to Chapel Street,
but that an iron grill stretches from wing to wing and
keeps out the town. This grill is high enough for

Hagenbeck, and it used to be a favorite game with us to play animal behind it for the street's amusement. At the hour when the crowd issued from the matinée at the Hyperion Theatre, our wittiest students paced on all fours up and down behind this grill and roared for raw beef. E—— was the wag of the building and he could climb up to a high place and scratch himself like a monkey—an entertainment of more humor than elegance. Elated with success, he and a companion later chartered a street-organ—a doleful one-legged affair—and as man and monkey they gathered pennies out Orange Street.

I turned into the dark Campus by Osborn Hall. It is as ugly a building as one could meet on a week's journey, and yet by an infelicity all class pictures are taken on its steps. Freshman courses are given in the basement—a French class once in particular. Sometimes, when we were sunk dismally in the irregular verbs, bootblacks and old-clothes men stopped on the street and grinned down on us. And all the dreary hour, as we sweated with translation, above us on the pavement the feet and happy legs of the enfranchised went by the window.

Yale is a bad jumble of architecture. It is amazing how such incongruous buildings can lodge together. Did not the Old Brick Row cry out when Durfee was built? Surely the Gothic library uttered a protest against its newer adjunct. And are the Bicentennial buildings so beautiful? At best we have exchanged the fraudulent wooden ramparts of Alumni Hall for the equally fraudulent inside columns of these newer buildings. It is a mercy that there is no style and changing fashion in elm trees. As Viola might have remarked about the Campus: it were excellently done, if God did all.

Presently in the dark I came on the excavations for the Harkness quadrangle. So at last Commons was gone. In that old building we ate during our impoverished weeks. I do not know that we saved much, for we were driven to extras, but the reckoning was deferred. There was a certain tutti-frutti ice-cream, rich in ginger, that has now vanished from the earth. Or chocolate éclairs made the night stand out. I recall that one could seldom procure a second helping of griddlecakes except on those mornings when there were ants in the syrup. Also, I recall that sometimes there was a great crash of trays at the pantry doors, and almost at the instant two old Goodies, harnessed ready with mops and pails, ran out and sponged up the wreckage.

And Pierson Hall is gone, that was once the center of Freshman life. Does anybody remember *The Voice?* It was a weekly paper issued in the interest of prohibition. I doubt if we would have quarreled with it for this, but it denounced Yale and held up in contrast the purity of Oberlin. Oberlin! And therefore we hated it, and once a week we burned its issue in the stone and plaster corridors of Pierson.

There was once a residence at the corner of York and Library where Freshmen resided. The railing of the stairs wabbled. The bookcase door lacked a hinge. Three out of four chairs were rickety. The bath-tub, which had been the chemical laboratory for some former student, was stained an unhealthy color. If ever it shall appear that Harlequin lodged upon the street, here was the very tub where he washed his clothes. Without caution the window of the bedroom fell out into the back yard. But to atone for these defects, up through the scuttle in the hall there was an airy perch upon the roof. Here Freshmen might smoke their pipes in safety—a privilege denied them on the street—and debate upon their affairs. Who were hold-off men! Who would make Βουλη! Or they invented outrageous names for the faculty. My dear Professor Blank, could you hear yourself described by these young cubs through their tobacco smoke, your learned ears, so alert for dactyl and spondee, would grow red.

Do Scott's boys, I wonder, still gather clothes for pressing around the Campus? Do they still sell tickets—sixteen punches for a dollar—five punches to the suit? On Monday mornings do colored laundresses push worn baby-carts around to gather what we were pleased to call the "dirty filth"? And do these same laundresses push back these selfsame carts later in the week with "clean filth" aboard? Are stockings mended in the same old way, so that the toes look through the open mesh? Have college sweeps learned yet to tuck in the sheets at the foot? Do old-clothes men—Fish-eye? Do you remember him?—do old-clothes men still whine at the corner, and look you up and down in cheap appraisal? Pop Smith is dead, who sold his photograph to Freshmen, but has he no successor? How about the old fellow who sold hot chestnuts at football games—"a nickel a bush"—a rare contraction meant to denote a bushel—in reality fifteen nuts and fifteen worms. Does George Felsburg still play the overture at Poli's, reading his newspaper the while, and do comic actors still jest with him across the footlights?

Is it still ethical to kick Freshmen on the night of Omega Lambda Chi? Is "nigger baby" played on the Campus any more? The loser of this precious game, in the golden days, leaned forward against the wall with his coat-tails raised, while everybody took a try at him with a tennis ball. And, of course, no one now plays "piel." A youngster will hardly have heard of the game. It was once so popular that all the stone steps about the college showed its marks. And next year we heard that the game had spread to Harvard.

Do students still make for themselves oriental corners with Bagdad stripes and Turkish lamps? Do the fair fingers of Farmington and Northampton still weave the words " 'Neath the Elms" upon sofa pillows? Do Seniors still bow the President down the aisle of Chapel? Do students still get out their Greek with "trots"? It was the custom for three or four lazy students to gather together and summon up a newsy to read the trot, while they, lolling with pipes on their Morris chairs, fumbled with the text and interlined it against a loss of memory. Let the fair-haired goddess Juno speak! Ulysses, as he pleases, may walk on the shore of the loud-sounding sea. Thereafter in class one may repose safely on his interlineation and snap at flies with a rubber band. This method of getting a lesson was all very well except that the newsy halted at the proper name. A device was therefore hit on of calling all the gods and heroes by the name of Smith. Homeric combat then ran like this: *the heart of Smit was black with anger and he smote Smit upon the brazen helmet. And the world grew dark before his eyes, and he fell forward like a tower and bit the dust and his armor clanked about him. But at evening, from a far-off mountain top the white-armed goddess Smit-Smit* (Pallas-Athena) *saw him, and she felt compash—compassion for him.*

And I suppose that students still sing upon the fence. There was a Freshman once, in those early nights of autumn when they were still a prey to Sophomores, who came down Library Street after his supper at Commons. He wondered whether the nights of hazing were done and was unresolved whether he ought to return to his room and sit close.

Presently he heard the sound of singing. It came from the Campus, from the fence. He was greener than most Freshmen and he had never heard men sing in four-part harmony. With him music had always been a single tune, or at most a lost tenor fumbled uncertainly for the pitch. Any grunt had been a bass. And so the sound ravished him. In the open air and in the dark the harmony was unparalleled. He stole forward, still with one eye open for Sophomores, and crouched in the shadowy angle of North Middle. Now the song was in full chorus and the branches of the elms swayed to it, and again a bass voice sang alone and the others hummed a low accompaniment.

Occasionally, across the Campus, someone in passing called up to a window, "Oh, Weary Walker, stick out your head!" And then, after a pause, satirically, when the head was out, "Stick it in again!" On the stones there were the sounds of feet—feet with lazy purpose—loud feet down wooden steps, bound for pleasure. At the windows there were lights, where dull thumbs moved down across a page. Let A equal B to find our Z. And let it be quick about it, before the student nod! And to the Freshman, crouching in the shadow, it seemed at last that he was a part of this life, with its music, its voices, its silent elms, the dim buildings with their lights, the laughter and the glad feet sounding in the dark.

I came now, rambling on this black wintry morning, before the sinister walls of Skull and Bones.

I sat on a fence and contemplated the building. It is as dingy as ever and, doubtless, to an undergraduate, as fearful as ever. What rites and ceremonies are held within these dim walls! What awful celebrations! The very stones are grim. The chain outside that swings from post to post is not as other chains, but was forged at midnight. The great door has a black spell upon it. It was on such a door, ironbound and pitiless, that the tragic Ygraine beat in vain for mercy.

It is a breach of etiquette for an undergraduate in passing even to turn and look at Bones. Its name may not be mentioned to a member of the society, and one must look furtively around before pronouncing it. Now as I write the word, I feel a last vibration of the fearful tremor.

Seniors compose its membership—fifteen or so, and membership is ranked as the highest honor of the college. But in God's name, what is all this pother? Are there not already enough jealousies without this one added? Does not college society already fall into enough locked coteries without this one? No matter how keen is the pride of membership, it does not atone for the disappointments and the heart-burnings of failure. It is hinted obscurely for expiation that it and its fellow societies do somehow confer a benefit on the college by holding out a reward for hard endeavor. This is the highest goal. I distrust the wisdom of the judges. There is an honester repute to be gained in the general estimate of one's fellows. These societies cut an unnatural cleavage across the college. They are the source of dishonest envy and of mean lick-spittling. For three years, until the election is announced, there is much playing for position. A favored fellow, whose election is certain, is courted by others who stand on a slippery edge, because it is known that in Senior elections one is rated by his association. And is it not preposterous that fifteen youngsters should set themselves above the crowd, wear obscure jewelry and wrap themselves in an empty and pretentious mystery?

But what has this rambling paper to do with a pair of leather suspenders? Nothing. Nothing much. Only, after a while, just before the dawn, I came in front of the windows of a cheap haberdasher. And I recalled how I had once bought at this very shop a pair of leather suspenders. They were the only ones left—it was hinted that Seniors bought them largely—and they were a bargain. The proprietor blew off the dust and slapped them and dwelt upon their merits. They would last me into middle age and were cheap. There was, I recall, a kind of tricky differential between the shoulders to take up the slack on either side. Being a Freshman I was prevailed upon, and I bought them and walked to Morris Cove while they creaked and fretted. And here was the

very shop, arising in front of me as from times before
the flood. With it there arose, too, a recollection of
my greenness and timidity. And mingled with all
the hours of happiness of those times there were
hours, also, of emptiness and loneliness—hours when,
newcome to my surroundings, for fear of rebuff I
walked alone.

The night still lingers. These dark lines of wall
and tree and tower are etched by Time with memories
to burn the pattern. The darkness stirs strangely,
like waters in the solemn bowl when a witch reads off
the future. But the past is in this darkness, and the
December wind this night has roused up the summer
winds of long ago. In that cleft is the old window.
Here are the stairs, wood and echoing with an almost
forgotten tread. A word, a phrase, a face, shows for
an instant in the shadows. Here, too, in memory, is
a pageantry of old custom with its songs and uproar,
victory with its fires and dance.

Forms, too, I see bent upon their books, eager or
dull, with intent or sleepy finger on the page. And
I hear friendly cries and the sound of many feet
across the night.

Dawn at last—a faint light through the elms.
From the Chapel tower the bells sound the hour and
strike their familiar melody. Dawn. And now the
East in triumphal garment scatters my memories,
born of night, before its flying wheel.

Boots for Runaways.

NOT long ago, having come through upon the uppers of my shoes, I wrapped the pair in a bit of newspaper and went around the corner into Sixth Avenue to find a cobbler. This is not difficult, for there are at least three cobblers to the block, all of them in basements four or five steps below the sidewalk. Cobblers and little tailors who press and repair clothing, small grocers and delicatessen venders—these are the chief commerce of the street. I passed my tailor's shop, which is next to the corner. He is a Russian Jew who came to this country before the great war. Every Thursday, when he takes away my off suit, I ask him about the progress of the Revolution. At first I found him hopeful, yet in these last few months his opinions are a little broken. His shop consists of a single room, with a stove to heat his irons and a rack for clothes. It is so open to the street that once when it was necessary for me to change trousers he stood between me and the window with one foot against the door by way of moratorium on his business. His taste in buttons is loud. Those on my dinner coat are his choice—great round jewels that glisten in the dark.

Next to my tailor, except for a Chinese laundry with a damp celestial smell, is a delicatessen shop with a pleasant sound of French across the counter. Here are sausages, cut across the middle in order that no one may buy the pig, as it were, in its poke. Potato salad is set out each afternoon in a great bowl with a wooden spoon sticking from its top. Then there is a baked bean, all brown upon the crust, which is housed with its fellows in a cracked baking dish and is not to be despised. There is also a tray of pastry with whipped cream oozing agreeably from the joints, and a pickle vat as corrective to these sweets. But behind the shop is the bakery and I can watch a wholesome fellow, with his sleeves tucked up, rolling pasties thin on a great white table, folding in nuts and jellies and cutting them deftly for the oven.

Across the street there resides a mender of musical instruments. He keeps dusty company with violins and basses that have come to broken health. When a trombone slips into disorder, it seeks his sanitarium. Occasionally, as I pass, I catch the sound of a twang-

ing string, as if at last a violin were convalescent.
Or I hear a reedy nasal upper note, and I know that
an oboe has been mended of its complaint and that
in these dark days of winter it yearns for a woodside
stream and the return of spring. It seems rather a
romantic business tinkering these broken instruments
into harmony.

Next door there is a small stationer—a bald-headed
sort of business, as someone has called it. Ruled
paper for slavish persons, plain sheets for bold
Bolshevists.

Then comes our grocer. There is no heat in the
place except what comes from an oil stove on which
sits a pan of steaming water. Behind the stove with
his twitching ear close against it a cat lies at all hours
of the day. There is an engaging smudge across his
nose, as if he had been led off on high adventure to
the dusty corners behind the apple barrel. I bend
across the onion crate to pet him, and he stretches his
paws in and out rhythmically in complete contentment. He walks along the counter with arched back
and leans against our purchases.

Next our grocer is our bootblack, who has set up
a sturdy but shabby throne to catch the business off
the "L." How majestically one sits aloft here with
outstretched toe, for all the world like the Pope
offering his saintly toe for a sinner's kiss. The robe
pontifical, the triple crown! Or, rather, is this not
a secular throne, seized once in a people's rising?

Here is a use for whatever thrones are discarded by this present war. Where the crowd is thickest at quitting time—perhaps where the subway brawls below Fourteenth Street—there I would set the German Kaiser's seat for the least of us to clamber on.

I took my shoes out of their wrapper. The cobbler is old and wrinkled and so bent that one might think that Nature aimed to contrive a hoop of him but had botched the full performance. He scratched my name upon the soles and tossed them into the pile. There were big and little shoes, some with low square heels and others with high thin heels as if their wearers stood tiptoe with curiosity. It is a quality, they say, that marks the sex. On the bench were bits of leather, hammers, paring-knives, awls, utensils of every sort.

On arriving home I found an old friend awaiting me. B—— has been engaged in a profitable business for fifteen years or so and he has amassed a considerable fortune. Certainly he deserves it, for he has been at it night and day and has sacrificed many things to it. He has kept the straight road despite all truant beckoning. But his too close application has cramped his soul. His organization and his profits, his balance sheets and output have seemed to become the whole of him.

But for once I found that B—— was in no hurry and we talked more intimately than in several years. I discovered soon that his hard busyness was no more than a veneer and that his freer self still lived, but in confinement. At least he felt the great lack in his life, which had been given too much to the piling up of things, to the sustaining of position—getting and spending. Yet he could see no end. He was caught in the rich man's treadmill, only less horrible than that of the poor man with its cold and hunger.

Afterwards, when he had gone, I fell into a survey of certain other men of my acquaintance. Some few of them are rich also, and they heap up for themselves a pile of material things until they stifle in the midst. They run swiftly and bitterly from one appointment to another in order that they may add a motor to their stable. If they lie awake at night, they plan a new confusion for the morrow. They are getting and spending always. They have been told many times that some day they will die and leave their wealth, yet they labor ceaselessly to increase their pile. It is as if one should sweat and groan to load a cart, knowing that soon it goes off on another road. And yet not one of these persons will conceive that I mean him. He will say that necessity keeps him at it. Or he will cite his avocations to prove he is not included. But he plays golf fretfully with his eye always on the score. He drives his motor furiously to hold a schedule. Yet in his youth many of these prosperous fellows learned to play upon a fiddle, and they dreamed on college window-seats. They had

time for friendliness before they became so busy holding this great world by its squirming tail.

Or perhaps they are not so *very* wealthy. If so,
they work the harder. To support their wives and
children? By no means. To support the pretense
that they are really wealthy, to support a neighbor's
competition. It is this competition of house and
goods that keeps their noses on the stone. Expendi-
ture always runs close upon their income, and their
days are a race to keep ahead.

I was thinking rather mournfully of the hard and
unnecessary condition of these persons, when I fell
asleep. And by chance, these unlucky persons, my
boots and my cobbler, even the oboe mender, all of
them somehow got mixed in my dream.

It seems that there was a cobbler once, long ago,
who kept a shop quite out of the common run and
marvelous in its way. It stood in a shadowy city over
whose dark streets the buildings toppled, until spiders
spun their webs across from roof to roof. And to
this cobbler the god Mercury himself journeyed to
have wings sewed to his flying shoes. High patron-
age. And Atalanta, too, came and held out her swift
foot for the fitting of a running sandal. But perhaps
the cobbler's most famous customer was a well-known
giant who ordered of him his seven-league boots.
These boots, as you may well imagine, were of prodigious size, and the giant himself was so big that
when he left his order he sat outside on the pavement

and thrust his stockinged foot in through the window for the cobbler to get his measure.

I was laughing heartily at this when I observed that a strange procession was passing by the cobbler's door. First there was a man who was burdened with a great tinsel box hung with velvet, in which were six plush chairs. After him came another who was smothered with rugs and pictures. A third carried upon his back his wife, a great fat creature, who glittered with jewels. Behind him he dragged a dozen trunks, from which dangled brocades and laces. This was all so absurd that in my mirth I missed what followed, but it seemed to be a long line of weary persons, each of whom staggered under the burden of an unworthy vanity.

As I laughed the night came on—a dull hot night of summer. And in the shop I saw the cobbler on his bench, an old and wrinkled man like a dwarf in a fairy tale. There was a sign now above his door. "Boots for Runaways," it read. About its margin were pictures of many kinds of boots—a shoe of a child who runs to seek adventure, Atalanta's sandals, and sturdy boots that a man might wear.

And now I saw a man coming in the dark with tired and drooping head. In both hands he clutched silver pieces that he had gathered in the day. When he was opposite the cobbler's shop, the great sign caught his eye. He wagged his head as one who comes upon the place he seeks. "Have you boots for me?" he asked, with his head thrust in the door.

"For everyone who needs them," was the cobbler's answer.

"My body is tired," the man replied, "and my soul is tired."

"For what journey do you prepare?" the cobbler asked.

The man looked ruefully at his hands which were still tightly clenched with silver pieces.

"Getting and spending," said the cobbler slowly.

"It has been my life." As the man spoke he banged with his elbow on his pocket and it rattled dully with metal.

"Do you want boots because you are a coward?" the cobbler asked. "If so, I have none to sell."

"A coward?" the man answered, and he spoke deliberately as one in deep thought. "All my life I have been a coward, fearing that I might not keep even with my neighbors. Now, for the first time, I am brave."

He kicked off his shoe and stretched out his foot. The cobbler took down from its nail his tape line and measured him. And the twilight deepened and the room grew dark.

And the man went off cheerily. And with great strides he went into the windy North. But to the South in a slow procession, I saw those others who bore the weary burden of their wealth, staggering beneath their load of dull possessions—their opera boxes, their money-chests and stables, their glittering houses, their trunks of silks and laces, and on their backs their fat wives shining in the night with jewels.

On Hanging a Stocking at Christmas.

AS Christmas is, above all, a holiday for children, it is proper in its season to consider with what regard they hold its celebration. But as no one may really know the secrets of childhood except as he retains the recollection of his own, it is therefore in the well of memory that I must dip my pen. The world has been running these many years with gathering speed like a great wheel upon a hill, and I must roll it backward to the heights to see how I fared on the night and day of Christmas.

I can remember that for a month before the day I computed its distance, not only in hours and minutes but even in seconds, until the answer was scrawled across my slate. Now, when I multiply 24 x 60 x 60, the resulting 86,400 has an agreeable familiarity as the amount I struck off each morning. At bedtime on Christmas Eve I had still 36,000 impatient seconds yet to wait, for I considered that Christmas really started at six o'clock in the morning.

There was, of course, a lesser celebration on Christmas Eve when we hung our stockings. There were six of them, from mother's long one to father's short one. Ours, although built on womanish lines, lacked the greater length and they were, consequently, inferior for the purpose of our greed; but father's were woefully short, as if fashioned to the measure of his small expectancy. Even a candy cane came peeping from the top, as if curiosity had stirred it to look around.

Finally, when the stockings were hung on the knobs of the mantel, we went up the dark stairs to bed. At the landing we saw the last glimmer from the friendly sitting-room. The hall clock ticked solemnly in the shadow below with an air of firmness, as much as to say that it would not be hurried. Fret as we might, those 36,000 seconds were not to be jostled through the night.

In the upper hall we looked from a window upon the snowy world. Perhaps we were too old to believe in Santa Claus, but even so, on this magic night might not a skeptic be at fault—might there not be a chance that the discarded world had returned to us? Once a year, surely, reason might nod and drowse. Perhaps if we put our noses on the cold glass and peered hard into the glittering darkness, we might see the old fellow himself, muffled to his chin in furs, going on his yearly errands. It was a jingling of sleigh bells on the street that started this agreeable suspicion, but, alas, when the horse appeared, manifestly by his broken jogging gait he was only an earthly creature and could not have been trusted on the roof. Or the moon, sailing across the sky, invited the thought that tonight beyond the accustomed hour and for a purpose it would throw its light across the roofs to mark the chimneys.

Presently mother called up from the hall below. Had we gone to bed? Reluctantly now we began to thumb the buttons. Off came our clothes, both shirts together tonight for better speed in dressing. And all the night pants and drawers hung as close neighbors, one within the other, with stockings dangling at the ends, for quick resumption. We slipped shivering into the cold sheets. Down below the bed, by special permission, stood the cook's clock, wound up tight for its explosion at six o'clock.

Then came silence and the night. . . .

Presently, all of a sudden, Brrr--! There arose a deafening racket in the room. Had the reindeer come afoul of the chimney? Had the loaded sleigh crashed upon the roof? Were pirates on the stairs? We awoke finally, and smothered the alarm in the pillows. A match! The gas! And now a thrill went through us. Although it was still as black as ink outside, at last the great day of all the year had come.

It was, therefore, before the dawn that we stole downstairs in our stockings—dressed loosely and without too great precision in our hurry. Buttons that lay behind were neglected, nor did it fret us if a garment came on twisted. It was a rare tooth that felt the brush this morning, no matter how it was coddled through the year.

We carried our shoes, but this was not entirely in

consideration for the sleeping house. Rather, our
care proceeded from an enjoyment of our stealth; for
to rise before the dawn when the lamps were still
lighted on the street and issue in our stockings, was
to taste adventure. It had not exactly the zest of
burglary, although it was of kin: nor was it quite
like the search for buried treasure which we played
on common days: yet to slink along the hallway on
a pitch-black Christmas morning, with shoes dangling
by the strings, was to realize a height of happiness
unequaled.

Quietly we tiptoed down the stairs on whose steep
rail we had so often slid in the common light of day,
now so strangely altered by the shadows. Below in
the hall the great clock ticked, loudly and with satisfaction that its careful count was done and its seconds
all despatched. There was a gurgle in its throat
before it struck the hour, as some folk clear their
throats before they sing.

As yet there was not a blink of day. The house
was as black as if it practiced to be a cave, yet an
instinct instructed us that now at least darkness was
safe. There were frosty patterns on the windows of
the sitting-room, familiar before only on our bedroom
windows. Here in the sitting-room arose dim shapes
which probably were its accustomed furniture, but
which to our excited fancy might be sleds and veloci-
pedes.

We groped for a match. There was a splutter that showed red in the hollow of my brother's hand.

After the first glad shock, it was our habit to rummage in the general midden outside our stockings. If there was a drum upon the heap, should not first a tune be played—softly lest it rouse the house? Or if a velocipede stood beside the fender, surely the restless creature chafed for exercise and must be ridden a few times around the room. Or perhaps a sled leaned against the chair (it but rested against the rigors of the coming day) and one should feel its runners to learn whether they are whole and round, for if flat and fixed with screws it is no better than a sled for girls with feet tucked up in front. On such a sled, no one trained to the fashions of the slide would deign to take a belly-slammer, for the larger boys would cry out with scorn and point their sneering mittens.

The stocking was explored last. It was like a grab-bag, but glorified and raised to a more generous level. On meaner days shriveled grab-bags could be got at the corner for a penny—if such mild fortune fell your way—mere starvelings by comparison—and to this shop you had often trotted after school when learning sat heaviest on your soul. If a nickel had accrued to you from the sale of tintags, it was better, of course, to lay it out in pop; but with nothing better than a penny, there was need of sharp denial. How you lingered before the horehound jar! Coltsfoot, too,

was but a penny to the stick and pleased the palate.
Or one could do worse than licorice. But finally you
settled on a grab-bag. You roused an old woman
from her knitting behind the stove and demanded that
a choice of grab-bags be placed before you. Then,
like the bearded phrenologist at the side-show of the
circus, you put your fingers on them to read their
humps. Perhaps an all-day sucker lodged inside—
a glassy or an agate—marbles best for pugging—or
a brass ring with a ruby.

Through the year these bags sufficed, but the
Christmas stocking was a deeper and finer mystery.
In the upper leg were handkerchiefs from grand-
mother—whose thoughts ran prudentially on noses—
mittens and a cap—useful presents of duller purpose—things that were due you anyway and would
have come in the course of time. But down in the
darker meshes of the stocking, when you had turned
the corner of the heel, there were the sweet extras of
life—a mouth-organ, a baseball, a compass and a
watch.

Some folk have a Christmas tree instead of hanging their stockings, but this is the preference of older
folk rather than the preference of children. Such
persons wish to observe a child's enjoyment, and this
is denied them if the stocking is opened in the dawn.
Under a pretense of instruction they sit in an absurd
posture under the tree; but they do no more than
read the rules and are blind to the obscurer uses of

the toys. As they find occasion, the children run off
and play in a quieter room with some old and broken
toy.

Who can interpret the desires of children? They
are a race apart from us. At times, for a moment,
we bring them to attention; then there is a scurry of
feet and they are gone. Although they seem to sit
at table with us, they are beyond a frontier that we
cannot pass. Their words are ours, but applied to
foreign uses. If we try to follow their truant
thoughts, like the lame man of the story we limp behind a shooting star. We bestow on them a blind
condescension, not knowing how their imagination
outclimbs our own. And we cramp them with our
barren learning.

I assert, therefore, that it is better to find one's
presents in the dawn, when there is freedom. In all
the city, wherever there are lights, children have
taken a start upon the day. Then, although the toys
are strange, there is adventure in prying at their
uses. If one commits a toy to a purpose undreamed
of by its maker, it but rouses the invention to further
discovery. Once on a dark and frosty Christmas
morning, I spent a puzzling hour upon a coffee-
grinder—a present to my mother—in a delusion that
it was a rare engine destined for myself. It might
have been a bank had it possessed a slot for coins.
A little eagle surmounted the top, yet this was not a
sufficient clue. The handle offered the hope that it

was a music-box, but although I turned it round and round, and noises issued from its body quite foreign to my other toys, yet I could not pronounce it music. With sails it might have been a windmill. I laid it on its side and stood it on its head without conclusion. It was painted red, and that gave it a wicked look, but no other villainy appeared. To this day as often as I pass a coffee-grinder in a grocer's shop I turn its handle in memory of my perplexing hour. And even if one remains unschooled to the uses of the toys, their discovery in the dawn while yet the world lies fast asleep, is far beyond their stale performance that rises with the sun.

And yet I know of an occurrence, to me pathetic, that once attended such an early discovery. A distant cousin of mine—a man really not related except by the close bond of my regard—was brought up many years ago by an uncle of austere and miserly nature. Such goodness as this uncle had once possessed was cramped into a narrow and smothering piety. He would have dimmed the sun upon the Sabbath, could he have reached up tall enough. He had no love in his heart, nor mirth. My cousin has always loved a horse and even in his childhood this love was strong. And so, during the days that led up to Christmas when children speculate upon their desires and check them on their fingers, he kept asking his uncle for a pony. At first, as you might know, his uncle was stolid against the thought, but finally, with many winks and nods—pleasantries beyond his usual habit—he assented.

Therefore in the early darkness of the day, the child came down to find his gift. First, probably, he went to the stable and climbing on the fence he looked through the windows for an unaccustomed form inside the stalls. Next he looked to see whether the pony might be hitched to the post in front of the house, in the manner of the family doctor. The search failing and being now somewhat disturbed with doubt, he entered his nursery on the slim chance that the pony might be there. The room was dark and he listened on the sill, if he might hear him whinny. Feeling his way along the hearth he came on nothing greater than his stocking which was tied to the andiron. It bulged and stirred his curiosity. He thrust in his hand and coming on something sticky, he put his fingers in his mouth. They were of a delightful sweetness. He now paused in his search for the pony and drawing out a huge lump of candy he applied himself. But the day was near and he had finished no more than half, when a ray of light permitted him to see what he ate. It was a candy horse—making good the promise of his uncle. This and a Testament had been stuffed inside his stocking. The Testament was wrapped in tissue, but the horse was bitten to the middle. It had been at best but a poor substitute for what he wanted, yet his love was so broad that it included even a sugar horse; and this, alas, he had consumed unknowing in the dark. And even now when the dear fellow tells the story after these many years have passed, and comes to the sober end with the child crying in the twilight of the morning, I realize as not before that there should be no Christmas kept unless it be with love and mirth.

It was but habit that we hung our stockings at the chimney—the piano would have done as well—for I retain but the slightest memory of a belief in Santa Claus: perhaps at most, as I have hinted, a far-off haze of wonder while looking through the window upon the snowy sky—at night a fancied clatter on the roof, if I lay awake. And therefore in a chimney there was no greater mystery than was inherent in any hole that went off suspiciously in the dark. There was a fearful cave beneath the steps that mounted from the rear to the front garret. This was wrapped in Cimmerian darkness—which is the strongest pigment known—and it extended from its mouth beyond the furthest stretch of leg. To the disillusioned, indeed, this cave was harmless, for it merely offset the lower ceiling of the bathroom below; yet to us it was a cave unparalleled. Little by little we ventured in, until in time we could sit on the snug joists inside with the comfortable feeling of pirates. Presently we hit on the device of hanging a row of shining maple-syrup tins along the wall outside where they were caught by the dusty sunlight, which was thus reflected in on us. By the light of

these dim moons the cave showed itself to be the size
of a library table. And here, also, we crouched on
dark and cloudy days when the tins were in eclipse,
and found a dreadful joy when the wind scratched
upon the roof.

In the basement, also, there was a central hall that
disappeared forever under an accumulation of porch
chairs and lumber. Here was no light except what
came around two turns from the laundry. Even
Annie the cook, a bold venturesome person, had
never quite penetrated to a full discovery of this hallway. A proper approach into the darkness was on
hands and knees, and yet there were barrels and
boxes to overcome. Therefore, as we were bred to
these broader discoveries, a mere chimney in the
sitting-room, which arose safely from the fenders, was
but a mild and pleasant tunnel to the roof.

And if a child believes in Santa Claus and chimneys, and that his presents are stored in a glittering
kingdom across the wintry hills, he will miss the finer
pleasure of knowing that they are hidden somewhere
in his own house. For myself, I would not willingly
forego certain dizzy ascents to the topmost shelves of
the storeroom, where, with my head close under the
ceiling and my foot braced against the wall, I have
examined suspicious packages that came into the
house by stealth. As likely as not, at the ringing of
the door-bell, we had been whisked into a back room.
Presently there was a foot sounding on the stairs and

across the ceiling. Then we were released. But something had arrived.

Thereafter we found excitement in rummaging in unlikely places—a wary lifting of summer garments laid away, for a peek beneath—a journey on one's stomach under the spare-room bed—a pilgrimage around the cellar with a flaring candle—furtive explorations of the storeroom. And when we came to a door that was locked—Aha! Here was a puzzle and a problem! We tried every key in the house, right side up and upside down. Bluebeard's wife, poor creature,—if I read the tale aright,—was merely seeking her Christmas presents around the house before the proper day.

The children of a friend of mine, however, have been brought up to a belief in Santa Claus, and on Christmas Eve they have the pretty custom of filling their shoes with crackers and scraps of bread by way of fodder for the reindeer. When the shoes are found empty in the morning, but with crumbs about—as though the hungry reindeer spilled them in their haste—it fixes the deception.

But if one must have a Christmas tree, I recommend the habit of some friends of mine. In front of their home, down near the fence, is a trim little cedar. T—— connects this with electric wires and hangs on it gayly colored lamps. Every night for a week, until the new year, these lights shine across the snow and are the delight of travelers on the road. The

Christmas stars, it seems, for this hallowed season have come to earth.

We gave the family dinner. On my mother fell the extra labor, but we took the general credit. All the morning the relatives arrived—thin and fat. But if one of them bore a package or if his pockets sagged, we showed him an excessive welcome. Sometimes there was a present boxed and wrapped to a mighty bulk. From this we threw off thirty papers and the bundle dwindled, still no gift appeared. In this lay the sweetness of the jest, for finally, when the contents were shriveled to a kernel, in the very heart of it there lay a bright penny or common marble.

All this time certain savory whiffs have been blowing from the kitchen. Twice at least my mother has put her head in at the door to count the relatives. And now when the clock on the mantel strikes two—a bronze Lincoln deliberating forever whether he will sign the Emancipation Bill—the dining-room door is opened.

The table was drawn out to prodigious length and was obliquely set across the room. As early as yesterday the extra leaves had been brought from the pantry, and we had all taken part in fitting them together. Not to disturb the larger preparation, our supper and breakfast had been served in the kitchen. And even now to eat in the kitchen, if the table is set before the window and there is a flurry of snow outside, is to feel pleasantly the proximity of a great occasion.

The Christmas table was so long and there were so many of us, that a few of the chairs were caught in a jog of the wall and had no proper approach except by crawling on hands and knees beneath it. Each year it was customary to request my maiden aunt, a prim lady who bordered on seventy and had limbs instead of legs, to undertake the passage. Each year we listened for the jest and shouted with joy when the request was made. There were other jests, too, that were dear to us and grew better with the years. My aunt was reproved for boisterous conduct, and although she sat as silent as a mouse, she was always warned against the cider. Each year, also, as soon as the dessert appeared, there was a demand that a certain older cousin tell the Judge West story. But the jest lay in the demand instead of in the story, for although there was a clamor of applause, the story was never told and it teases me forever. Then another cousin, who journeyed sometimes to New York, usually instructed us in the latest manner of eating an orange in the metropolis. But we disregarded his fashionable instruction, and peeled ours round and round.

The dinner itself was a prodigious feast. The cook-stove must have rested and panted for a week thereafter. Before long, Annie got so red bringing in turkeys and cranberry sauce—countless plates heaped and toppling with vegetables and meats—that one might think she herself was in process to become a pickled beet and would presently enter on a platter.

In the afternoon we rested, but at night there was a dance, for which my maiden aunt played the piano. The dear good soul, whose old brown fingers were none too limber, had skill that scarcely mounted to the speed of a polka, but she was steady at a waltz. There was one tune—bink a bunk bunk, bink a bunk bunk—that went around and around with an agreeable monotony even when the player nodded. There was a legend in the family that once she fell asleep in the performance, and that the dancers turned down the lights and left the room; to her amazement when presently she awoke, for she thought she had outsat the party.

My brother and I had not advanced to the trick of dancing and we built up our blocks in the corner of the room in order that the friskier dancers might kick them over as they passed. Chief in the performance was the Judge West cousin who, although whiskered almost into middle age, had a merry heart and knew how to play with children. Sometimes, by consent, we younger fry sat beneath the piano, which was of an old square pattern, and worked the pedals for my aunt, in order that her industry might be undivided on the keys. It is amazing what a variety we could cast upon the waltz, now giving it a muffled sound, and presently offering the dancers a prolonged roaring.

Midway in the evening, when the atrocities of dinner were but mildly remembered, ice-cream was brought in. It was not hard as at dinner, but had settled to a delicious softness, and could be mushed upon a spoon. Then while the party again proceeded, and my aunt resumed her waltz, we were despatched upstairs.

On the bed lay our stockings, still tied with string, that had been stuffed with presents in the dawn. But the morning had now sunk into immeasurable distance and seemed as remote as Job himself. And all through the evening, as we lay abed and listened to the droning piano below, we felt a spiritual hollowness because the great day had passed.